The InnerKinetics® of Type

Sixteen Variations of Temperament

More on how we are designed from

Ray W. Lincoln

The InnerKinetics® of Type

Sixteen Variations to Temperament

Paperback ISBN: 978-0-9842633-0-1

LCCN: 2012949207

Ɑpex Publications
Littleton, Colorado

Dedication

Once again I am indebted to the many I have met and sought to help in one way or another. All have sharpened my understanding of that amazing creation we call people. Learning will never end. The path to self-understanding is still being explored but the knowledge that began two and one half millenniums ago is still the most valid path to self-knowledge: temperament and type.

All of us are not only the subjects of temperament study but also the contributors, teachers, and exponents. So, to all of us who are collectively called people, this book is dedicated.

> I wish I loved the human race;
> I wish I loved its silly face;
> I wish I liked the way it walks;
> I wish I liked the way it talks;
> And when I'm introduced to one
> I wish I thought, what jolly fun.
> ~ Walter Raleigh -

> It *is* fun!
> ~ Ray W. Lincoln -

Contents

Appendix I: The Temperament Key for Adults

Appendix II: Short Descriptions of Each Temperament

Preface

Why This Book?

Do you want to know everything you can about yourself or those close to you? If you do, this book will take you beyond the understanding of your temperament to the understanding of your type. It is your introduction to type — a deeper understanding of how you are so uniquely and wonderfully designed. It's true that we don't understand ourselves or others like we should, and ever since David Keirsey and Marilyn Bates published *Please Understand Me*, people seem to realize they should pay more attention to understanding and appreciating the most complex and complicated organism in the universe: you and all *Homo sapiens*.

There are four temperaments that we refer to as SP, SJ, NT, and NF. Each of these has four variations and we call these variations *types.* But why do you need to know your type? Because it will tell you more about how you are made and fine-tune your knowledge of a fulfilling direction for your life. It will help you know why you do what you do and assist you to manage your needs and potentials with greater skill. You have only one life to live. Live it to the fullest. Learn, gather information, understand what you know, and be wise.

Knowing who we are is important if we want to be the best we can be. But also knowing who others are enables us to help them in a way that those who do not understand them cannot. This book will take you on a tour of the sixteen types made famous by Myers-Briggs to increase your knowledge of people and your people skills. However, it will do so with the positive principles of understanding built into InnerKinetics®.

This book is a supplement to *INNERKINETICS* by Ray W. Lincoln. InnerKinetics® is a study of the four temperaments and how life can be changed by self-understanding and the application of that knowledge. Please read *INNERKINETICS* since it is the foundational knowledge to making the most of this book. If you are coaching others this book has also been written for you so that you can connect with your clients on a deeper level of recognition and comprehension.

You probably know people who represent a number of the types. Seeing people act out their type or fight with themselves, trying to be someone else, is fascinating and educational. However, if you want to help others, especially your child, the knowledge of type, which is merely a name for the variations found in each temperament, is paramount. There are many more benefits than simply understanding yourself, your child or others. Chapter 1 will let you into those secrets.

Take the exciting journey into the mysteries and raptness of who you are "on the inside" and you will, I promise, never be the same again. Your life will throb with positive pleasure and new horizons when you correctly perceive yourself.

Introduction

A man of understanding shall attain unto wisdom.
~ Proverbs 1:5

You may have picked up this book with an understanding of what it's all about. If not, ask yourself, "Do I really understand myself and others? That is, do I really understand why they act and feel and think the way they do?" Is there someone that seems totally weird to you or even so unlike you that you can't understand them? If there is, you are reading an eye-opener. This book is about understanding people in more detail than only understanding their temperament (one of four) can do for you. It will help you understand how people of the same temperament differ and you can become an expert at using that knowledge to benefit all of us.

First, have an eye-opening experience by taking the Adult Temperament Key in Appendix I and look hard and long at yourself in the brief descriptions you will find in Appendix II of this book and the detailed ones in *INNERKINETICS*. You have been made wonderfully. Believe that! If you don't like what you see it is because you are not appreciating your strengths and realizing how much the world needs them and you. Only if you are who you are made to be will you find a life of real happiness and fulfillment. Discovering who we are can feel like a release from prison, the prison of our own misunderstanding and downgrading of ourselves.

People, including yourself at times, are not easy to understand. They all seem somewhat different and even if you understand the four temperaments (the fast and user-friendly way of understanding people), you may still notice that people of the same temperament seem different in some ways and similar in others. Is there any more help? Yes, each temperament, as I have said, is divided into four types or variations. Each type or variation of a temperament shares the same basic temperament but shows distinct differences in the expression of that temperament with some added elements. This is where this book will take you: into the variations within a temperament to see others and ourselves in a more erudite and expansive way. You will be equipped

having or showing
great knowledge or learning

with all you need to know about yourself and to find your way with success and pleasure through the days of your life.

In understanding others, you will discover why the ESTJ seems so controlling and the ESFJ runs around trying to provide for everyone's needs; why the ESFP is a real performer and loves the limelight and why the ISFP shrinks from the limelight but still loves to creatively have an impact on people. Two are SJs (ESTJ and ESFJ) and two are SPs (ESFP and ISFP), yet see how differently they express their temperament. Perhaps you will appreciate what understanding your type will do for you if you know how to use this book for its greatest benefit.

How to Use This Book

Use it to deepen your understanding of yourself

Take the journey few take and learn how you are made. Like so many who have read *INNERKINETICS*, you may have another amazing "Aha" moment as you discover your type. There is a sense of relief in realizing why you do what you do and feel what you feel. As we have said, you may have already observed that you are different from others or maybe you see it as them being different from you. Whatever. Understanding the forces and drives of not only your temperament but also of your type, which creates yet more preferences, will open up the path to making changes you have wanted to make but didn't know why you couldn't seem to make them or how to make them.

So, use this book for self-understanding, self-improvement, self-actualization, and for reaching your potential. Always begin by studying yourself. The mystery of others is then understood against the backdrop of how you feel, think, act and find fulfillment and happiness.

Use it to deepen your understanding of your child and other people in your life

We are often puzzled by the behavior of others and judge them by our own feelings and preferences. This, as you may have observed, does not improve relationships. People want to be understood — not through your filter but through theirs. Along with *INNERKINETICS* this book will give you what you need to know to understand others. Instead of, "That's not the way to...," you will find yourself saying, "I think I understand why you do that. You are different from me and see things differently."

Your children long for you to understand them. They will only bond with those they feel comfortable with and those who they feel understand them. It makes sense for them to keep their distance from those who don't understand them. That way they protect themselves from those who condemn them without cause. And if you understand the deep drives inside of them that make them do what they do and feel what they feel, they will let you into the inner sanctum of their lives. Do you want that kind of acceptance? Use the knowledge you are given here, which is the result of observation and research that has been compiled for over two millenniums about who people are, and you will be approved by any child.

You will find your child verifying when you are right about how they feel and think, their preferences, and their goals. Their actions will tell you that you are connecting with them and their trust will confirm it even more. Whenever we read someone correctly, they benefit and so do we.

Use it as a reference book

Along with *INNERKINETICS,* you can use this book as a handy reference for all the purposes listed in Chapter 1, and more. There is nothing in life that is not affected by our drives and preferences. We choose based on them, and if we know them we can therefore recognize when we are choosing based on some other outside influence.

No doubt you will have many occasions when you will want to turn to your type and check to see if you are living to your potential. Remember, this is the foundational knowledge of how you are made. Type will not tell you if you should wear blue or red, but it will tell you, for example, if you are in the right career.

Sometimes we choose to act a certain way, even when it feels uncomfortable, because we feel pressured to do so. Sometimes we have been persuaded to act in a way of which we really do not approve. We make choices all the time and we need to know when we are choosing based on what is *us* or what is not *us*. Learning your type will help greatly. Also, all teens can steer their lives with greater wisdom when they know why they feel what they feel, what is truly them and what is not, and when their choices are or are not damaging to their happiness.

However, if you use this book as a reference to help you understand others, please don't use it as a weapon to correct others. They must self-understand and most of the time, with understanding, self-correct. We are not in this life to control other people or be their judges, but we are here to help each other and the distinction is super important. Just because some people use this knowledge to control others is no reason for us to decide not to understand other people. The misuse of knowledge is no reason to remain ignorant. Email can be misused to abuse others, but it is no reason to stop using email. Use this book to help others and, in particular, to help you appreciate where they are coming from.

Use It as a Relationship Guide

You now know that everyone is not like you. No big surprise. You have probably thought that some people are "strange," "unbelievable," "too emotional," or "too cold," and some just seem to come from another planet. Or, if it is your child, he was dropped off by the stork in the wrong home. So, imagine how two people who are different can get into all kinds of scrapes because they feel the other person is wrong in the way they deal with things. Some married people can't understand why they made the choice they did. "What happened?, or "Is there something missing in the relationship?" they ask. Are they wrong in having certain expectations of the other person and insisting on things being done the way it makes sense to them? In any relationship, we need to get along with others. How?

You are not the only person on this planet and the key is always to start with understanding why the others act differently. Appreciation and love depend on understanding, and because of understanding we also find it easier to forgive. Even tolerance is easier when we understand. Certainly, a love that understands is stronger glue than one that doesn't.

Along with *INNERKINETICS*, use this book as a guide to understanding those you love and those you don't. Partners who truly understand each other and use the knowledge to correct themselves succeed in making a great relationship. We can only change ourselves, so get busy on the task we all have to face and use this knowledge to accept and love others.

Use It as a Manual for Advice and Counsel

If you counsel or coach others, temperament and type is the place to start. Without understanding a person's tendencies, preferences, urges, and drives, you will not be able to help them as you wish, nor will they feel comfortable with you. They may put up with you since you are, in their minds, the expert, but that is far from a mutually understanding relationship. You will fail at making sense to them when you really need to. We are constantly hearing from professionals how an understanding of temperament and type changed their effectiveness and success in counseling.

Perhaps the biggest reason for this is the ability we have to motivate people when we truly understand their basic drives and urges. A depressed person is best helped when the therapist presents cognitive exercises and tasks according to how the person is naturally made to respond. Then they feel they can make changes. Some therapists don't know how their clients feel and think and prefer to act. Motivation is the great key to successfully helping people. So, let's lay a good foundation of how people are made and how they function. When we get it right, motivating a patient or client is comparatively easy.

Whatever is the need, understanding the person comes first since we are complex creatures with emotional forces that mold and make us. Type will open up a world of help. This volume and *INNERKINETICS* are used as two of the texts in my InnerKinetics® Level Two training courses. (You can learn about the training at www.raywlincoln.com.)

Here's the Journey We Will Take

Part 1 gives some guidance on how to use type in personal and professional settings. Chapter 1 looks at the benefits of applying the understanding of type to many circumstances common to most of us.

Chapter 2 gives us some of the benefits of applying our knowledge of type and the huge difference it can make to our personal growth and our relationships. We also go out into the real world by using a case study to show how application of the knowledge of type can be so helpful.

The letters used to designate the type can help with understanding the type. In the third chapter, we compile a list of the likely behavior we will find from each letter. Becoming familiar with these letters and their likely actions can help us draw some quick conclusions about the meaning of the type. The limitations of this speedy approach are discussed.

Chapter 4 asks whether there is any difference in the way a type is expressed in a child as opposed to an adult. Parents will need to study the comments in this chapter to understand their children.

Part 2 is the description of what has been known in temperament study as the sixteen types. Also, you will find invaluable help in the sections at the end of each description that indicate some areas for personal growth, notes on the child of this type, the effects and reduction of stress, and the feared Achilles heel. A summary for quick identification closes the explanation of each type. This is the major part of the book and you will no doubt find yourself returning to it many times and using it for reference purposes.

Appendices will help you by providing the Adult Temperament Key and a brief description of the temperaments so that you can confirm that your answers to the questions in the temperament key truly define who you are. For a fuller treatment of the temperaments and their strengths, I advise you to go to *INNERKINETICS*. Certainly if you are doubtful of your temperament you will need to refer to *INNERKINETICS*.

There is no better place to begin solving the problems of life and realizing the path to a fulfilling happiness than a complete understanding of how we are intricately designed.

Part 1: Using Type in Real Life

Temp + type are the
internal urges that move
or motivate us in a particular
direction.

1 — A Lifetime of Benefits

Man is the only creature who refuses to be what he is.
~ Albert Camus

The above quote is a sorry comment on how we humans have lived our lives. We want more than an academic knowledge of ourselves; we want results in our lives if the study of type is to mean anything and if we are to be motivated to be all we can be. What results can we expect? What challenges in life will the understanding of type profitably address? What difference will it make?

The possibilities of applying the knowledge of temperament and type to life seem almost unlimited and the benefits more wonderful than we can expect. Here are a few of the areas in which understanding our temperament and our type will be invaluable, and how it will be of value. If you are a therapist or counselor of any sort, each area we discuss briefly will offer help for your client.

Motivation

You know those flat times when you feel useless and worthless, don't you? How do you get out of them and feel again as though you are alive? The word motivation comes from the Latin "to move." Movement can be healing, stimulating, and therapeutic. What it does for the body it also does for the human spirit. We are designed to move and all of us know what happens when we avoid moving and exercising.

Motivation starts with internal urges that encourage us to do something pleasing and self-satisfying or something that propels us toward our goals. The inbuilt urges of the strengths of our temperament create our strongest motivations. (For a discussion of these strengths, see "Introduce Yourself to Your Strengths" in *INNERKINETICS*.) Temperament and type determine how we are best motivated and that's why we need the most intimate knowledge of our type.

Look at the description of your type and find the things that motivate and please you. These are the levers to use when you want to be lifted out of your depression. Remember that motivation must be linked with pleasure and not with negative emotions, since moving is not helpful if it is in a damaging or wrong direction. Knowing your type will help you banish those demotivated, sad times and power yourself out of the doldrums.

Simply follow the urges of your temperament and type to be content, happy, and satiated. Motivation is a natural result of the application of our positive, inbuilt urges. Find those natural urges in your temperament and your type descriptions.

Finding Life's Purpose

Living with no purpose soon opens the door to feelings of uselessness, worthlessness, and despair. People become irritated, frustrated, angry, morose, and depressed when these feelings hit. Not just movement, but direction with purpose must be present in our lives for us to keep out of this pit of despair. Purpose keeps us focused and happiness is always found in a purposeful life. You probably know someone who, when their life seems to fall apart, remains focused and seems to be above the dark clouds, sailing along in the sunlight of a fixed purpose. We all wish to be like these purpose-driven, happy people.

Purpose and direction are not the same thing. We want to know *where* we are going (direction) and *why* we want to go there (purpose). *Where* and *why* are questions first answered by knowing how we are designed to function happily. Once we find our purpose, we often find our direction at the same time, but not always. So, to live with real contentment we need both our purpose and our direction to be clear and to become the foundation of our life's vision.

Where do we find our purpose? Purpose is discovered, just like motivation, in the strengths that we have been given. It is seen in our "design." The direction we seek is also found in our design. As we interact with our world, our environment often further defines us, and environmental situations are as endless as the possibilities that life presents.

4

Direction for our lives is first found in our purpose, and then we discover the way to our life's goals. Finding both the purpose and the direction, or the way they are to be expressed for us individually, is one of the most important tasks of life. We must start with understanding our temperament and type or we can be led astray on an unsatisfying goose chase. Are you beginning to see how important an understanding of how you are designed really is?

Developing Potential

Once we have found our purpose and direction in life, we need to develop our potential. Potential is the undeveloped ability to achieve a goal or complete a task. We can know our purpose and the way to it, but without developing our potential we can still fail to be fulfilled. The maximizing of our potential is found in the development of our strengths. Those strengths are our dominant urges. These urges need to become abilities or they can excite us but fail to move us.

The development of our potential involves finding the steps to the successful realization of our purpose. Those steps need to be motivating to us. We are best motivated by hope and mental force (determination) that is focused and involves steps we believe in.

We never go crazy about developing our potential if we don't have a vision or dream for our lives. There is no motivation in exercising if we don't have a reason and a goal that rewards our efforts. We exercise to lose weight, look good, feel healthy, gain energy, to enjoy the "high" it gives, etc. — never do we do it without a goal. We will develop our potential strengths and abilities if we have a dream crystalized by a finely tuned goal.

We don't have to feel comfortable about developing our potential. Doing what is uncomfortable, if we have a purpose that feels like it is truly us, becomes a challenge and we accept it as a necessary hill to climb. Development must sometimes also become discipline. "We cannot get what we've never had, unless we're willing to do what we've never done," author unknown. How true that is of building potential as well as the reaching of our goals.

5

Both temperament and type provide a guide to the development of our potential. Potential speaks of our power or potency. That power is generated by our focus, a focus that rewards and feels like it is truly us. This is what we will commit to. When we know and verify our type, we can draw from its descriptions to find the things that will empower us. Reading through a description of our type sparks ideas and reminds us of what energizes us.

Release from Our Concerns

Negative concerns that ruminate in our minds become millstones we drag through life. They can be things as simple as, "Why do I get so emotional and upset?" or perhaps "Why am I so unfeeling or coldhearted?" We are often concerned that there is something wrong with us when others criticize us and infer that we should be like them or deal with life like they do. Then we may read a description of our type and find it is how we are made. An "Aha" moment hits us and we have a tremendous sense of relief and a new perspective on our lives. We are all right after all. Introverts usually feel this relief more since they are usually criticized more.

We may also hate the detailed job we are in and then find out we are not made for details, rather for seeing and finding the big picture and forming the vision. The relief is great and the redirection of our lives is a Godsend. People often feel they are just starting to live when they discover themselves.

Self-discovery brings release from nearly all the concerns we have carried around with us that cause us to think we are not adequate or to ask "Why does my mind not seem to operate the way some other mind works? Am I mentally impoverished or slow?" We learn that the temperaments have different intelligences, and the types within a temperament have different usages and expressions of their temperament's intelligence. Welcome the joy of finding out how you are made, because your concerns may become reasons for happiness. Your strengths — not your weaknesses — are the topic of *INNERKINETICS*, and finding that what we once perceived as a weakness is instead a strength to be celebrated is a happy revelation. We discover all these things when we discover our type. Concerns are turned to revelations.

Learning

People don't all learn the same way. Temperament, as well as type, has a lot to do with it. If we are despairing because we just can't memorize like some others, we may find help in knowing that details are not our "thing." We can also discover how to learn those details and why we tend to have such trouble with them. The preferred methods of learning differ with temperament and type, so be sure to know, understand, incorporate, and apply your type's characteristics to your learning methods.

The characteristics of the type will indicate preferences in study habits and, for some types, the importance of atmosphere when they study. For example, introverts will mostly like solitude and enjoy in-depth analysis more, while the extroverts will enjoy group learning and interaction in the classroom. Extroverts will love to talk and think while they talk. Conversely, introverts will usually be silent and think before they feel they can say anything. Many other differences pervade the field of learning.

Those with a "T" in their profile will prefer facts and only facts, relating one fact to another with logic and sequence, while those with an "F" will want to know the meaning behind the facts and the emotional impact the facts might have on people. The "Ns" will progress in their thinking by observing patterns in the facts or data. They will not usually move sequentially through the facts in a step-by-logical-step procedure.

Study and learning comes naturally when we understand our design.

Loving

In romance, the desires and expressions of love can vary greatly even within a temperament. For example, the ESFJ has markedly different needs than the ISTJ, and the ENFP is more outwardly oriented in love than the INFP. Each letter will have something to say about how we love and want to be loved. Partners are often dumbfounded to learn that their spouse doesn't want to be loved in the same way they themselves do. Love also means something different from one type to another. An introverted lover wants something different out of love than an extroverted lover.

Without love all types wilt, but some wilt much quicker than others. Understanding a person's love needs and how they express love makes for a stronger bond among lovers. Intimacy is more meaningful and transforms the simple touch into a meaningful encounter for some and not for others.

Love depends on understanding and the more we understand, the closer the bond. We will not willingly and meaningfully give ourselves to those who do not understand us. Out of understanding each other's type comes respect and acceptance that makes each partner feel at home in the other's love. Is this a benefit?

Losing

Losses are inevitable in life. From simple failures, to guilt-ridden heartaches, to deep grief over the loss of a loved one, losses can cause severe tremors. Temperament and type are central to discovering the right methods for recovery and healing after loss.

Each type experiences loss in a different way marked by the differences in the letters. An extrovert who is an ST will grieve differently from an ENT or ENF or an ESF. The explanation of each type will capture these differences in the way the type prefers to act.

When an ESTP is given the same counseling to exit grief as an INFJ, for example, one or both are going to respond negatively and fail to be helped. This is true of nearly all the types. Fit the shoe to the foot or it will hurt and maybe create compounding hurts. Much damage has been done to grieving people whose type has not been taken into account in the selection of treatment therapies.

Perhaps in loss, the importance of understanding a person's deep urges and drives is highlighted, since success or failure depends so much on it. Why would we treat all cases of grief the same when we know each person is different? Yet, a set path to recovery is often all that is advocated.

Winning and Ecstasy

Perhaps we would think there couldn't be much difference between people when winning. They are all excited and pumped. Yes? True, but not true. One is in ecstasy and another is contented, two emotions that are poles apart in their intensity and expression.

Different temperaments will view winning through their different strengths: some through the thrill of a rising self-esteem (SPs) and others will value winning as less important because they (NFs) see it through a stronger surge of empathy for the loser.

Types also indicate differences. The ENFJ will let their friend win quicker, being more socially oriented than the INFJ, unless the INFJ feels guilty about something. The ENFPs will be more passionate about winning since they are the champion who want more to be in the winner's circle. And please note: all of these have the same temperament, just a difference in type. The INFP will even be more content than the other NFs to be the loser if it will heal a rift or bring wholeness to a relationship. From these surprising facts, the benefits of knowing our type should be self-evident.

SPs must win, but the ISFP (who is an SP, but in some respects quite different) may choose not to compete and be content in not competing. Winning stirs our emotions and these emotions mobilize some types more than others. Watch out, too, for the letdown after the ecstasy, which will even more dramatically show the differences in type and temperament.

Depression

It is in depression that extra care needs to taken to treat each person according to their type. Motivation is only achieved when we use our strengths and urges and function according to how we are designed. A depressed person is in need of all the motivation that can be mustered. To fail to do so is to fail them. Depression, of course, destroys motivation but motivation is one of the greatest needs. By nature, the longer a person is in depression, the more difficult it is to help them lift themselves out. A malfunctioning brain must be coaxed and prodded to function healthily and find motivation again before it can be restored to normality.

Extroverts and introverts are motivated and helped differently. "Ss" and "Ns" also have dramatically different ways of gathering data from the world as well as different methods for feeling the joy of life again differ. The same striking differences are true of the "Ts" and "Fs" and the "Js" and "Ps." The knowledge of temperament and type is a Godsend to the coach, therapist or counselor when facing a depressed person.

This fact influences all we can accomplish: namely, when we operate according to how we are made, we feel good, well, healthy, and rewarded. The aim of all who seek to help the depressed must include an understanding of the preferences and drives that move that person. The benefit of understanding type is, again, so evident.

Faith and Beliefs

Beliefs drive our actions. That's a huge statement. They can, among other things, strengthen our resolve and build our confidence. Of course, they can also do the opposite with destructive speed. It all depends on the nature of the belief. By now it is not surprising to find that the way we believe and how it has an impact on us is different with each type. Each type sees hope and optimism differently. Some are plagued by worry, some not. The extroverts in all temperaments view their beliefs with more optimism than the introverts, who need their beliefs to be more definite and clear-cut. NTs can't believe in anything that is not precise and logically tight. There are also motivations that drive us to believe or doubt that are unique to the way each type is made.

So, how we believe and with what intensity we believe differs from type to type. "Know yourself," said the ancient Greek philosophers. It is said of Jesus that he went everywhere preaching change and belief. All the great figures of history knew the power and potency that lay in their beliefs.

Here are some other factors in play with the types. All SJs are prone to negativity and doubt, but are propelled downward into anxiety for different reasons. Within the SJs, the ESTJ loses faith when they lose control; the ESFJ, when they fail to be successful providers, helpers, and social organizers; the ISTJ, when they fail to succeed at their watchfulness, and the ISFJ, when they fail to be able to help the downtrodden and protect them. Type matters in understanding the quirks of how we believe and the paths to and from it.

Focus

Focus has already been mentioned and perhaps should have been mentioned under all of these benefits. We are built to focus and without it, the effectiveness of eyesight is depleted and hearing is clouded. In fact, every sensory input and every mental capacity is lessened or eliminated if it has no focus. Now it may still come as a surprise to some that the focus of each type is also different. The reason lies in the fact that their interests and urges are different. We all need to focus on our life and our goals or life passes us by, leaving none of its rewards and treasures behind.

Focus deepens on a target that is identified. When driving down the road, we (hopefully) look at something, not nothing, for example. Knowing our type helps us select targets that will be in-sync with our design. We will, when we are aware, naturally select the things that follow our drives and cause us to use our strengths.

The sharper our focus, the more we can create intense energy. The mind's focus is where the energy is instigated. To train ourselves to be well-focused and to know how and where we will find the most rewarding targets determines success for each of us in our own special way.

Choices and Preferences

Life is all about making the right choices. It's easy to say, isn't it? The tough part is in sorting through the many influences that want to get our vote and choosing the ones that fit us and make us grow. This is where values come in. What is it we value? Where do we invest our interest to stimulate wanted results?

The study of type again rewards us. Choosing according to the urges that are within us and acting without overusing them or misusing them is the path to being who we are and finding our nirvana. We must make right spiritual choices, career choices, relationship choices, and personal temperament and type choices.

Choosing a Mate

Let's talk a little more about this one. Should we choose a partner who is the same as us? The answer, surprisingly, is no! Two lives with the same preferences and urges might seem to be heaven on earth, but hell comes nearer as a description of the reality. Why? When two people who both have the same drives live in close relationship they enter into competition with each other. They compete for those feelings of self-worth that come from being superior or from winning, and the friction or competition can become unbearable. If each is in competition then someone must win. Relationships are not smooth in the stress of competition, nor do they blend.

If the partners are opposites, appreciation for the differences is essential for a happy relationship. Whenever two do not appreciate each other's differences, fights, accusations, and hurt abound. However, understanding someone and appreciating their type is not an impossible task unless we are over-inflated with our own importance; in which case, why do we need a relationship?

Before we choose a mate, understanding them and ourselves and the possible interactions between us is only wise. We should and can know where we will blend harmoniously, where we will clash, and what we can do about those issues to encourage a blending. Furthermore, we can have a glimpse of our future. All of this is provided with a careful study of each person's type. A huge benefit to any relationship, don't you think?

Solving Relationship Issues

Pleasant relationships make life enjoyable. Once we are in a relationship, are we doomed to whatever the match offers? No! Most relationship problems stem first from a misunderstanding or non-understanding of each other. Even financial problems and the friction caused by different values and preferences over money start with not understanding correctly why each sees money and its demands differently and why it raises their concern.

Some types are free with money; others hold it with clenched fist. Some are generous and others are saving every penny for a rainy day. Some want to take risks and if they are not responding to the risk, they feel they are cowardly. Other types are nervous, even paranoid, about taking risks of any sort. The starting place for finding solutions to all relationship problems is to see that in a blend of opposites, each must understand and respect the urges of the other.

But relationships are not all about money. Love is uppermost. Each type gives love in a slightly different manner, as we have discussed, so the solutions are always found in understanding the love life and personal preferences of both partners.

Self Development

Although all we have said about the benefits of understanding our type has something to do with personal growth, it deserves to be mentioned separately. If we don't grow, what happens to our lives? They don't just stagnate — they decline and decay. Just like a 12-year-old infant is a sad abnormality, so a 50-year-old man who has the maturity of a 20-year-old is sad and regrettable too.

Self-development begins with self-understanding. Do all you can to know all you can about yourself, and then you can mature with wisdom and experiences relevant to your dreams.

Self Image

Confidence in ourselves is not pride. Confidence is an ingredient in making good choices and in being wisely decisive. Without a healthy, confident self-image we are limited in our growth. Courage is a central factor in success and living without it creates timid, wimpy people.

Courage begins with what we think about our abilities and ourselves. That's what self-image is all about. Therefore, a sound, healthy self-esteem leads the way to being bold in our decisions: opportunists and entrepreneurs that make our way in life. Both dependence and independence are needed at the right times and in the choices we make. Knowing who we are and what we can and cannot successfully achieve gives us this confidence to be both dependent and independent at the right times. Self-knowledge is an essential step to a strong self-image.

These are some of the benefits of knowing our type. They are also some of the areas in which we can profitably use type. Add your own areas of concern. Take any area in which you want to achieve and go to your type description. Start reading in the lines and between the lines. You will find what and how you can best do what you want to do, using the elements of your own design to empower you.

2 — Out in the Real World

The more one judges, the less one loves.
~ Honore de Balzac, *Physiologie du Mariage*

Out there in the real world people clash and misunderstand each other, causing all kinds of distress. They also love and appreciate each other. Sometimes they stumble on success in their relationships and sometimes they needle and frustrate each other with anger and hurt, creating violent eruptions. Most of the trouble can be explained as a clash, and the acceptance as an understanding of our differences. When we know what is happening inside another person and why they are doing what they are doing, life becomes more manageable, tolerant, and forgiving.

So, learning your type is not just a matter of knowing your letters. To say "I'm an ESFJ" is not to know anything if we don't know how to apply the knowledge to what is happening in our lives. The following case study, changed a little to protect the couple, may help us understand how to use the information from the descriptions of the types in Part 2. A practical view of how type helps may illuminate how to interpret the knowledge you will receive in Part 2.

Let's find out what it looks like when we fail to understand and then when we understand. Here's how it worked out for Trish and John in their relationship.

Trish and John

We will call the wife (who is an ENFP), Trish, and the husband (who is an ISTJ), John. Trish works at home taking care of the kids. John owns and manages an appliance store and works long hours at times. They have been married for nine years.

Trish is sensitive and John knows that but does not know why. "She's a woman," he says to his buddies. But that's not a good enough explanation. Not all women are sensitive. He has a mental set that thinks they are, but he hasn't paid any real close attention to the matter. Every time she gets hurt, he puts it down to her sensitivity and her being a woman. John is not very sensitive at all. He has emotions that can be deeply stirred, but he engages them very little in comparison to Trish.

It was her birthday and he forgot to say "Happy Birthday." He bought a new fridge a month ago and casually remarked that it was a birthday present. "That was generous, wasn't it?" he later explained to his mates. He also came in from work the day he had forgotten her birthday and decided she needed to be told to get the kids to pick up their toys. "The house is a mess," he scolded. He never noticed her withdraw and inwardly seethe with hurt and sadness. It was a cool, quiet evening that followed as Trish buried herself in Facebook, while texting and receiving birthday wishes and chatter from one of her close girlfriends. The feelings of being unimportant to John, of rank disharmony, and of a dozen other emotions emanating from hurt were inflaming her mind.

It's getting late and John tries to give her a kiss as he saunters off to bed, but he notices her lips are as hard as stone. It's not the first time he has felt the cool granite of unwilling lips, so he thinks little of it and puts it down to her sensitivity as he turns in for the night. He calls out in a commanding tone, "Come to bed!" Now the fires of Hell are burning hot.

At around two A.M. he wakes up and she isn't in bed. He feels the first tinge of real concern. He finds her on the couch asleep and wakes her. He is mystified at why she is there. He never has understood her. Why she does what she does — he just doesn't get it. She is dismissive and curt and tells him to go away and leave her alone. He's heard that tone before so he submits and returns to bed.

Days go by and he is shut out of her heart. He feels it and clams up too, and decides not to communicate, not knowing what he can say, as he puts it, that will not make her more angry. He reasons that if she doesn't want to talk he is not going to force her. Besides, he's angry too. At last he becomes really concerned and asks, "When are you going to change your mood?"

That does it. Days of pent-up hurt and anger erupt in a withering verbal blast of hate from Trish. All her accusations burst out and she finally says, "I'm not sure I can stand this relationship; I don't mean anything to you. I may as well not be here." He is stunned and disbelieving. What is she going to do? And then he makes his final mistake. He figures if he doesn't know what to say to fix it, he had best say nothing, and he withdraws further into himself, saying to himself, "I guess it's over between us."

Let's use the understanding of type and see what he misunderstood, what she did not do that she should have, and the reasons why.

Solutions for the Real World

John knows Trish is sensitive but he could have known, if he understood her type, that hers is a sensitivity beyond his experience of sensitiveness. It is a dominant drive and strength in her. The emotional surges of hurt capture the ENFP and the one who hurts them must show some sort of concern when the ENFP suddenly acts withdrawn or angry. He did not show this because he did not have an understanding of her type. John could have gone to her and apologized saying, "If I have hurt you in any way I am deeply sorry. Please tell me what I have or haven't done." ENFPs respond to that soft approach. If he had done this he would have been told, "You haven't wished me a happy birthday. That fridge is for the house, not for me. And why are you policing me and judging me the moment you come through the door? You treat me as a chattel, not a wife. I don't seem to matter at all to you."

Equally, if Trish had known that John was not as sensitive as she was and that he gets lost in worry and concern, acting like the commander of the house when he is living in his weaknesses, she could have told him that his barking at her was not the action of someone who cared for his wife. She could have told him the rest of his failures, giving him the opportunity to do what was right and prove his love if it was there). Type would have told her all of this.

John had a long way to go to make her feel loved again now. John, of course, may have felt she was making a mountain out of a molehill. But wait. When another person feels hurt, it is not about who's acting right but about healing and love, which we all tend to forget. Later, when calm, they each could discuss their needs and requests for how they want to be treated and could learn to respect each other.

The ENFP lives for the meaning of the moment, and her birthday moment now had bad meanings. He has, at best, inadvertently robbed her of pleasure on the moment of her birthday. If he knew her type he would have known it was time for a lot of making up, or the ENFP would sink into self-blame.

Even though Trish is an extrovert and loves to be around people, children do not recharge an extroverted NF like adults do. She was also drained from all the conflicts and disharmonies of the day. She had been waiting for his loving surprise, but his tone of voice when he barked at her told her none was coming. This is another hurt: the loss of an important expectation. ENFPs are devastated when reasonable expectations are dashed.

He paid no attention to her coldness and withdrawal, which he would have known were the NF's red flags had he understood her type. ENFPs are warm and vivacious when happy. Stony lips told him she was upset and she knew that he knew something was wrong, but he did nothing because, at best, he didn't know what to do. Hard lips are a sign of disconnectedness and that's the ENFP's Achilles heel — the most damaging and difficult thing for them to handle. He didn't know that. To say nothing is an ISTJ's typical response when they feel they can't fix things. She didn't know that either. John must know, however, that he must treat the ENFP as an ENFP and not as an ISTJ. We can remain ourselves, but we need to treat people according to who *they* are if we want to succeed.

At two A.M. she told him to go away and leave her alone. The emotional message was clearly that of an NF who is deeply hurt. She then exploded on him and he still did nothing really significant to rectify matters.

Trish must learn that her hurt stirred her anger and that whenever she is angry she must do the right thing. Withdrawing and freezing are not positive solutions to her hurt or productive of harmony in the relationship. Knowing his tendency to forget romantic things when he is worried, she could have gently reminded him after telling him his comment about the children's toys was equally his responsibility. "Go ahead and pick them up or get the kids to do it," she could have said. The right thing for Trish to do was to take a time out and think of a positive response to the whole situation, giving her the best chance at controlling her emotions.

This is what it's like out there and can be like out there. Only an understanding of each other's type would have given Trish and John all this information. People respect others much easier when they understand them. They forgive more readily and are more tolerant and accepting. Whenever we look at another person it helps to conjure up a mental picture of the words written on their foreheads: "Please, understand me." If you believe, as many do, that we are made in the image of God, then it is essential we respect and attempt to understand all people. All faiths have some call to treat others with integrity. Society falls apart without it.

Most problems can be solved with understanding, and those that can't require that we begin with understanding. Temperament is the best user-friendly way of understanding others, since it requires a knowledge of only four temperaments. Type is the best, detailed method to understand others and requires we know the temperament and its variation — its types.

3 — Letters and Their Message

Nothing in life is to be feared, it is only to be understood.
~ Marie Curie

A type is represented by letters (for example: ESTP). When trying to grasp the character of a type, it may help to watch for the expression of its elements: the characteristics of each of its letters. These typical elements are listed below to give us a quick understanding of what to expect from each letter. Don't think you have to memorize these, although it can put you in the ballpark of understanding a type when you are familiar with them. The meaning of the letters and the addition of two letters (E and I) also explain why there are variances (types) within a temperament.

These lists are no substitute for the descriptions of the sixteen types in Part 2. No attempt has been made here to make the lists complete as this might be impossible given the infinite expressions of our emotions and our strengths. Emotions give unique expressions to the strengths. Rather, they are representative of the most common tendencies of each letter and how they might affect the construction of the type.

Note also that each type will express these elements in different degrees of intensity and for different purposes. A parent, teacher, counselor — anyone — can grasp an understanding of a type more easily, even when a person is in a meltdown, when at least some of these elements are kept in mind.

In temperament analysis, each of these letters represents a finding in one of four categories. The E and I answer the question "How do we replenish our inner energies when we are drained?" The S and N indicate how we gather our information from the world. The T and F reveal how we make our decisions about the information we gather, and the J and P describe the lifestyle we favor.

The sum of the meaning of each letter does not fully describe the type. For example, an ESTP is not the sum of its letters, E+S+T+P = ESTP. Each letter reacts on the others and they condition each other. This complication again explains why we can be a certain type and yet be a unique expression of that type. So, to accurately describe the ESTP we must rely on the research that has been refined over the centuries, allowing for individual uniqueness. Hence, for a reliable and full understanding of each type, read the descriptions in Part 2. They have been formed from the efforts of many scholars over a long time. Verification by a person acts like the consent of the individual that they are being understood.

Also, remember that the four basic temperaments represented by two letters (SP, SJ, NT or NF) form the core or center of the type. The temperament lays the foundation for the type. We must always first understand the temperament and then the type. Start with identifying the temperament from the four letters. If the person is an SP temperament, those letters will occur in the four-letter profile. Likewise for the SJ, NT, and NF temperaments. The temperaments and their strengths are fully described in *INNERKINETICS*. Again, always start with the temperament and then proceed to the fuller description of the four letters, the type.

Here is your shorthand for the likely expression of each of the letters:

(E) Extrovert
(Compare each number with the same number under Introvert)

1. Oriented to the outside world — external
2. Recharge from engaging with people and things outside of themselves
3. Energy is directed outwardly
4. More easily read by others
5. Activity stimulates them
6. Socially stimulating to others
7. Seek interaction
8. Talkative
9. Open to outside stimuli

10. More tolerant of loud noises and of crowds
11. Easily distracted
12. Enjoy the spotlight
13. Restless if not engaged
14. Make fast first evaluations
15. Speak then think, or speak and think as they talk
16. Many relationships
17. Gregarious
18. Intelligence favors breadth and inclusiveness

(I) Introvert
(Compare each number with the same number under Extrovert)

1. Oriented to the inner world of mind — internal
2. Recharge from inner energies
3. Energy is directed inward
4. Not easily read by others
5. Quietness and solitude typically stimulates them
6. Socially reserved and shy
7. Want thinking time
8. Not talkative until they feel comfortable
9. Selective of outside stimuli
10. Loud noises and crowds disturb them
11. Strong focus
12. Enjoy solitude
13. Restless in social settings
14. Slower to evaluate
15. Think then talk
16. Fewer relationships
17. Retiring
18. Intelligence favors depth; reflection is essential

(S) Sensing
(Compare each number with the same number under Intuition)

1. Captured by the present moment
2. Reality
3. Details — precise information
4. Sequential
5. Observant, like firsthand experience
6. Focused on practicalities
7. Proceed step-by-step
8. Experience
9. Trust their five physical senses
10. Change when reality dictates
11. Perspiration
12. Actual — what is
13. Traditional
14. Down-to-earth
15. Fact

(N) Intuition
(Compare each number with the same number under Sensing)

1. Captured by what is possible
2. Fantasy
3. Concepts — ideas — the big picture
4. Mental leaps
5. Insightful, sensing the meanings
6. Focused on the theoretical, abstract, ingenious
7. Proceed randomly
8. Newness
9. Trust their intuition — gut feelings
10. Change when possibility calls
11. Inspiration
12. Possible — what might be, could be, should be
13. Creative
14. In-the-clouds

15. Meaning

(T) Thinking
(Compare each number with the same number under Feeling)

1. Logical, reasonable
2. Fast decisions
3. Downplays emotion
4. Objective
5. Critical, pointing out the negative
6. Justice
7. Laws
8. Truth
9. Policy, procedure, principle
10. Not personal
11. Skeptical, questioning
12. Detached
13. Wants clarity
14. Wants precision
15. Coldhearted
16. Head

(F) Feeling
(Compare each number with the same number under Thinking)

1. Emotions must count in any decision
2. Take time to process their feelings
3. Highlights emotions
4. Subjective
5. Forgiving and lenient, wants to focus on the positive
6. Mercy
7. Exceptions; laws don't cover every situation
8. Love
9. Values and priorities

10. Personal
11. Credulous
12. Attached and needing closeness
13. Harmony and agreement
14. Wants significance
15. Warmhearted
16. Heart

(J) J lifestyle
(Compare each number with the same number under P lifestyle)

1. Wants control over life, imposes their will on life
2. Sense of urgency
3. Must come to closure
4. Move on
5. Fixed
6. Planned
7. Deadline
8. Definite
9. Structure
10. Enjoy finishing things
11. Scheduled
12. Routine
13. Order, everything in its place
14. What is right
15. Purposeful

(P) P lifestyle
(Compare each number with the same number under J lifestyle)

1. Rather than control their world they observe it and experience it
2. Laid back
3. Keep options open
4. Wait

5. Adaptable and flexible
6. Spontaneous
7. When I am ready
8. Tentative
9. Go with the flow, tolerant
10. Enjoy starting things
11. Unscheduled
12. Change
13. Scattered
14. What is appropriate
15. In-the-moment

4 — Type as Seen in the Child

Furious activity is no substitute for understanding.
~ H. H. Williams

Train up a child in the way he should go and when he is old he will not depart from it.
~ Proverbs 22:6

Parents are keen to understand their children since there is no guarantee that the child will be like the parent. Is the expression of a type different in a child as compared to an adult? What should I, as a parent, be aware of in understanding my child?

Environment

The environment in which the child is being raised, either the home environment or the environment outside the home, may slow or speed up the development of the traits of the type. Always try to keep a positive, encouraging home environment for the healthy development of your child.

Your child may be trying to copy the way their friends or friends' parents are acting. If they are, this will appear as something not typical of their temperament and, therefore, if you know their type and temperament you can identify it as an adopted strength and encourage their given strengths. It is natural for a child to mimic others.

Environment, such as cultural differences, can influence a child to express their strengths in a different way from yours. This can happen if they have friends of another culture or if your child is adopted from another culture. Although it is the temperament that molds us, environment influences the way we express our preferences.

Development

Not necessarily everyone, child or adult, will have all the strengths of a temperament or the traits of a type, so don't look to develop all strengths of a given temperament or type. Develop the strengths they show an aptitude or liking for as you begin to observe them. They will also need to be taught to use their strengths and not to misuse them or overuse them. When teaching them, keep in mind that a positive approach from the parent as opposed to an accusing, condemning approach is always more effective and does not do damage.

The child will not typically develop all the strengths at once. When only an infant, one or a few of the strengths may progressively develop and more will show as the years go by. Watch with interest how your child's temperament and the individual traits of the child's type develop. You should be able to know the child's temperament for certain by two years of age, and the other elements of the type by no later than five. For many children, their full type will be evident before five years of age.

Determining and Developing a Strength

It would result in volumes of text to try to detail all the possible child expressions of each of the strengths and the traits, so let me give an example of one strength, which is a trait of the ESTP, as a guide to developing strengths: bravery.

Bravery can be seen in various ways. The child may be daring in some circumstances and cautious in others because the parent has modeled caution and/or the child has been deeply affected by some scary situation that left its mark. Underneath, if the child is an SP, the child will be daring, particularly when they are attempting something for which they do not have a troublesome memory. Look for what characterizes them and their preferences, not for their response to a single situation. Not all children are naturally brave and daring. Only the SP consistently exhibits this daring spirit, and the ESTP in spades. So look for consistency.

Each adult will have a different idea of what defines courage, bravery, and a daring behavior. An SP adult will have a different view from an SJ. Make your judgment according to the description in the temperament and type you suspect the child to be, and see if that judgment makes sense for that type. If you suspect the child to be an ESTP, look at them through the typical lens of an ESTP, the one described in that type, and make a judgment with that in mind.

FINAL TEST: Once you have made your best assessment, treat the child accordingly, and if the child responds favorably or shows that he is comfortable with it you will know you have come to the right conclusion.

If still confused, check with a trained InnerKinetics® coach. Only in rare occasions should this be necessary.

Part 2: The 16 Types

The Sixteen Types

Introduction

Everything that irritates us about others can lead us to an understanding of ourselves.
~ Carl Jung

I have endeavored over the last fifty years in particular to compile from the work of others and refine with my own observations a description of the sixteen types. My indebtedness to those who have already written reliable descriptions will be clear. Among them are Myers-Briggs, Keirsey, Berens, and a host of others. Repetition of facts and ideas that research has already unearthed is inevitable in a project that seeks to garner the wisdom of the ages.

I have also tried to express what I feel is the core of each type so that a picture of their main characteristics becomes clearer. No attempt is made to be exhaustive in listing all that could be said about each type. The variations between people would make this an impossible task, so the central themes of the type must suffice. Theories underlie the way InnerKinetics® sees each type, but the theory must not mold the facts. Rather, the other way around. Our personal observations will also expose the occasional exception to the rule since, to some extent, each description is a generalization. All of us are unique, but with all the research, we are able to describe a person accurately, if not completely.

At the end of each description you will find a section entitled **"Some Areas for Growth."** These are some of the main areas for development and may help you and your friends or clients.

How stress is experienced for each type is discussed under **"Stress for the...,"** and some ways to reduce or avoid it are suggested. The main concerns in parenting the child are also mentioned in the section entitled **"The Child,"** as well as a brief mention of **"The Achilles Heel"** that must be avoided at all costs.

The **"Summary"** at the end of each type's description gives you a handy, quick reference to the core of the type.

When learning the characteristics of the types, InnerKinetics® wants you first to be very familiar with the four temperaments — SP, SJ, NT, and NF — since the temperament is the core of the type's characteristics.

The SP Temperament

ESTP

ESTPs can **engage you** and hold your attention, perhaps like no other type. One of their great gifts is being able to make a presentation and **persuade people, showing a confidence that itself feels convincing**. They may not be as interested as other SPs at operating machinery, but they **operate people** with the s**moothness** of a skilled con artist and can manipulate anybody who is unaware of their intentions, especially those who tend to doubt themselves.

Not only people, but **solving any problem on the spot** stimulates them. They are fiercely focused on what is happening around them. They live in the moment always and they would ask, "Is there any other moment to live in?" Hence, they can easily forget the past because only the present and the very immediate future hold attraction. Being down-to-earth, the problems they solve are not of an abstract nature. Rather they concentrate on the practical ones.

People tend to be molded and shaped in their hands like clay in the hands of a skilled potter. This can lead to overconfidence on the part of the ESTP in dealing with people and can cause their downfall. They don't always succeed at manipulating people either, because the other temperaments have their own skills. The NT's defense against these smooth people-skills is their insistence that the suggestion must be rational or it doesn't make sense to do what the ESTP suggests. The NF's defense is a sharp intuition against being fooled, and the SJ's is their suspicious, cautious nature. However, it is hard to reject the social sophistication and political savvy of these types.

You might imagine that they are **pleasant,** with an attractive charm and wit, and you would be right. But there may be something else going on. With an engaging concentration on you, they can make you feel as if they are full of sympathy and concern for you and your cause, when in fact they are simply reading you like a book. Of course this is not what all ESTPs are doing all the time, but the skill is there.

Life is a constant round of **excitement and action** for the ESTP, which keeps them alert and happily savoring every moment. The ESTP craves action. It makes them feel the rush of adrenaline and the sensory pleasures of movement, stimulating their strong desire to live on the upside of life. Sports can attract them, of course, but doubly so if they have an audience and can feel the **impact** they are making. Action means **high energy** too, and to be without it is to be dead. They keep going until they drop, especially the young ones. You can always tell when they are asleep — when they stop moving.

They tend to live by the dictum "make hay while the sun shines" and can teach us how to live open to joy and all of its opportunities. **Handling the downside** when it becomes apparent that it is inevitable disturbs and puzzles them. They do not visit this side of life often by choice. A short-lived depression can lurk in its shadows for the ESTP.

Impressive is a good word to describe them and how they have an impact on others. They light up a room or excite a game, always on the lookout for the **winning edge**. Their minds are focused on results and, at times, it is for them the only thing that matters. Morals, ethics, manners, cultural norms, and the niceties of operation can fall by the wayside as they doggedly force their way to their goals. They will not bother to justify themselves; it's a waste of time — just move on.

If you have ever met a **high-roller,** he may have been an ESTP seeking to impress. New and dashing clothes, fancy restaurants, a love for all the richer, finer things of life — good food, fine wine, expensive toys — these can shape their adventures. They are not the only ones who love these things, but they see a purpose in them as well as pleasure.

Generosity can be a strong point. Easy come, easy go is how they think, and if you need something of theirs they will consider giving it to you. They can get more tomorrow. This confidence is based not only on a belief in a plentiful world but also in their ability to succeed. They seldom doubt themselves, breathing a spirit of hope in their actions and words. In return for their generosity, they would like to feel that you would reciprocate when needed.

Again, you might have surmised that they are **very observant**. They pick up physical and verbal cues that others, except for those with intuitive skills, never notice. They do not blink when facing indications of distaste or dislike in their audience. They simply search for the moment of acceptance. For them, it has to be there.

But included with all this are a powerful **extroverted optimism** and an expectant emotion that drives them more than any other SP. This also drives them to be **adaptable**. Change is almost worshipped. Also, with optimism comes a **daring** nature, exhibiting a bravery and courage that lives on the edge of danger or, for some, foolishness. If one option doesn't work there are always others. In their persistence to find a way, they can be ruthless. Somehow ESTPs believe they can talk and wriggle their way out of anything, and they usually do. **The edge of danger is exhilarating,** to say the least, so **risks** are all part of the game. Their fearlessness helps them overcome people who show hesitancy and doubt.

ESTPs hate to have to listen to long, drawn-out explanations. Of greater disdain to them are the meaningless theoretical surmises of philosophy or mathematics. If it has no immediate, practical application it is boring. But they are **tolerant** of others and their beliefs. Just don't try to force yours on them.

Their "come follow me" **leadership** makes them **somewhat distant** as friends, and they never really open their hearts for a true mutual discussion. Instead, they keep leading the charge and **living their fantasy with an earthbound reality.**

We need to note their great entrepreneurial abilities: always promoting themselves but at times impatient and overly aggressive. If the spotlight is taken from them, they may also show irritation or anger. The anger is short-lived and they seldom lose their focus when they have been sidetracked by anger.

Relationships can pose problems since they are seen as a kind of contract that binds the ESTP. They need freedom to move and explore the present moment. Long-term relationships may end up as a kind of negotiated freedom. If you can rope an ESTP as your partner and still give them reign to feel their freedom, they will make your life a never-ending round of fun, risk, and excitement.

Some Areas for Growth

- Open-mindedness. When making decisions, consider not only what you feel is relevant, but also think of what you may not consider relevant.
- Details. Pay attention to all the data or you may be processing only what interests you.
- Structure. Become more comfortable with structure and deadlines.
- Analysis. Develop a more far-reaching tactical assessment of all possibilities.
- Strengths. Live in the satisfaction of your strengths.
- Mental pace. Keep pace with other people's comprehension; don't race ahead of them.
- Understanding. Approach people on their values, not on your own.
- Emotions. Develop an awareness of other people's personal needs.
- Manipulation. Be careful not to appear manipulating.
- Relationships. Develop patience where relationships are a concern.
- Respect. Respect other people's feelings and needs.
- Self-image. Accept disagreement as another chance to win, not as a disappointment or rejection.
- Values. Develop a wisdom that gains more respect than materialistic trappings.

Stress for the ESTP

Loss of confidence caused by having to think of yourself less than optimistically will create a sudden stress factor and you will feel the unfamiliar emotions of inadequacy. In the extreme, it leads to depression. Effectiveness and success are the antidotes.

Because you live in the moment and whatever is taking your attention is dominating your mind, thinking well of yourself is achieved by getting out there and being who you are. It's a matter of feeling the lift of your strengths that cause you to make an impact and dominate the moment. This is the way out of depression: Live in the power of your strengths.

Sometimes the obstacles you face will be too great to overcome, such as a stubborn person who just won't let you control or influence them. It can also be an unexpected loss of resources or anything that makes you feel like you hit a wall and can't find a way around it. Stress will mount, as nothing you can see in the moment offers a solution. It leads to confusion and discouragement. Confusion fogs the mind and discouragement closes the mental doors to discovery. You can find yourself scrambling for the right action. At this point, you can overreact and do whatever comes to mind, probably doing the wrong thing and complicating the problem. Take time out or seek help and understanding. The stress has its resolution in a solution. Pause and analyze the realities of what you face. Act only when you know it is the best thing to do.

Stress can also result from feeling that you have lost your grip and others are now discrediting you or, worse, still ignoring you. These factors, too, are solved practically. You have not lost the strengths that make you successful; you simply have to refocus and find what will give you the opportunity to regain your lost esteem. You may need to admit your mistake and, if so, remember, that is a healthy way to regain your standing and confidence. Perhaps you were too optimistic and needed to factor in some realities that you could not change. To think you can do anything is good for your confidence, but you will have to, at times, confess to your limits. Perhaps the greatest limit is that you can't control other people if they don't want you to. You can only control yourself. All of us have limits; we are limited creatures.

On the whole, little will stress you because of your staunch optimism. Where others fold, you are likely to push ahead with your "take the reigns" attitude and your firm belief in the success of your tactical mind.

Remedies for stress are best found in your temperament's strengths: action, movement, finding the happiness of the moment, and lighthearted playfulness with others and with life. Operating these strengths and simply going out and making an impact are the most lasting and effective ways to deal with stress.

The Child

This child is likely to be very active. Efforts to impress their playmates will become increasingly obvious; so will their "come follow me" leadership. As they discover their strengths, they may tend to control by pressure rather than their tactical skills. Their tactical thinking and strategic cunning may at times surprise you. Watch for their apparent skill at purpose-driven scheming. The charm of the ESTP will also be obvious.

Their confidence and daring nature has to be watched or without the wisdom to know what is dangerous, they do themselves harm. Harm, however, will not necessarily dissuade them. The edge of danger appeals to them.

A lack of concentration is often noted, but it can be simply an interest in everything around them and a desire to impress whenever the opportunity arises. For most, few things will scare them and they will look for the winning edge in all encounters.

Adaptability should surface early, together with a love of change. The ESTP child is often willing to share, but expects the same in return.

If you are an SJ parent in particular, they can unnerve you with their high energy and daring nature. Direct their energy and their bravery. Don't try to suppress it or you will suffer the results of confronting a strength that just does not want to leave.

The Achilles Heel

These are the naturally optimistic ones. Not being able to make an impression after repeated attempts will either cause them to move on to impress another or fall into a mild depression. Unsuccessful behavior together with ineffectiveness can do the same. If they really do become chronically depressed it will destroy their optimistic self-image and the road back can be difficult. Getting them to succeed and lead again is the most potent remedy for their depression.

Central to helping an ESTP who has lost their motivation is to assist them in resetting their compass. They seek change and a re-calibrated direction for their goals will do wonders.

Summary

(This short summary can be a quick way of understanding the central themes of this type. Also, it can be used to check an assessment's accuracy by asking the person if they concur with a majority of these statements. Simply put, does it sound like them?)

ESTPs are natural "take charge" leaders and optimistic, smooth operators. Because of their tactical and persuasive skills, they like to be negotiators, watching with a sharp eye for any effective advantage. Their drive to win and succeed combined with a charismatic charm inspire confidence in them as well.

ESTPs can manipulate people with their engaging charisma. They keep their cool under pressure and operate freely without preconceived requirements. This means they must always keep their options open and are alert as consultants (a thing they also love to do) to all potentialities.

When needed, they can be aggressive, bold, flamboyant, and even lavish in their approaches. ESTPs also desire to be energetic, fun loving, and entertaining with a lust for living on the edge. Show them no respect and they wonder why they can't make an impressive impact.

ESFP

Showmanship ranks high as a skill and a fulfillment. ESFPs entertain from the very earliest of days to the end of their lives. Like all SPs, they are **full of fun** and always on a search for the last drop of excitement in the moment. Everything is a **performance,** from a child showing off how they floss their teeth to a Hollywood star. The world is a stage and life is "curtains up, curtains down," awaiting the applause. They feel a mission to lighten up the drab routines of life and lift others into the world of pleasure. Mischievous, talkative, infectious, and witty, they spice up the lives of all around them and take the center stage with obvious glee.

Many of them are talented in the **performing arts**. Dancing starts when only a year or two old, and the movement never stops. People love these **lighthearted, tolerant impressionists** who leave behind a wake that draws others in if only to have fun with them. Unlike the ESTP, who is the highlight of the evening, ESFPs hold the spotlight and perform in its light.

They preach a message of how humans must enjoy themselves and they gain an impressive congregation because of the woodenness of life's mundane demands and its cry for relief. Nothing to them is so sacred that it can't be made fun of, and the sacred itself is questionable because it feels alien to their message. "Don't inhibit me," they cry, and all that smacks of seriousness and caution puts the brake on their quest for fun.

Temptation is more of an enticement than a warning. Not that fun is evil. Joy is one of life's basic nutritional needs, but they don't seem to hear the call for restraint. For some of these **charming socialites,** "Eat, drink, and be merry" sums up the essence of living.

Company is a need, however. Aloneness is hell and the technology of our age that helps bridge the gap of distance is their godsend. If ever you need a **playmate,** this is one. Outgoing, accepting, and friendly, they like action and make things happen if the night-lights go dim.

Friends are not taken lightly. They make friendship a sacred trust, and only if you try to change them or they find a greater attraction will they break the tie. ESFPs are always on the lookout for a greater attraction. Relationships can be difficult to maintain if their interests wander too far. There is a **restlessness** in their spirit.

Therefore, standards, rules, commitments, and moral taboos can be lightly treated. What makes for a fun time and giving others a fun time is the prime motivation in these lovable playmates. They are very **observant** and read another's intentions with skill. **Emotions run deep** and they can recall them at will to reflect a character in their story or a memory that enriched them. When they feel impelled to speak their mind they are expressive with hot emotions, finding it hard to hold their tongue.

They have an eye for what impresses. **Flamboyant** and flirtatious, life is always a soap opera with its many changing characters. Their quick wit and piercing insight into what is working and what is not takes them far in the world of pleasure and action.

Generous to the core, they share willingly but expect you to do the same. As children, teaching them not to take another child's toy is difficult since they are willing for theirs to be shared. These restrictions make no sense in the free society of their minds.

ESFPs, like all SPs, like to make an impact, so the hot spots in town and the excitement of meeting people of notoriety stimulate them. As for all extroverts, but particularly the ESFP, **gatherings of any sort** can be an irresistible magnet. The thrill of drugs mixed with the desire to impress and the penchant for experimentation can make them sure candidates for substance abuse if they have not learned some self-discipline. That's a dirty word to them, of course, but essential to a small degree at least, to the ESFP.

Variety is a better word, and so is **optimism**. They share with the ESTP a belief that all that is can be changed and fashioned with the skills of a tactical mind, so why worry (another dirty word)? Anxiety destroys them more than any other type. Find the silver lining in the cloud and if you don't, it will find you, they believe. If you have a worry, ignore it until it won't be ignored, then find someone to help you make it go away. Although this overstates the attitude of some ESFPs, it is not far from the truth they feel in their hearts.

ESFPs are **warm, loving, and affectionate**. Their love is free with little demand in return. Sharing their lives with others seems only natural, but they share with a constant eye to making an impression. They join in with whatever is going on because they must feel the energy of others.

School is not their thing. The seriousness of learning what they feel is impractical and dull in the classroom ranks them with the other types that have more patience with recess. Reason is of a **practical, common sense** nature. Their minds turn quickly to the concrete facts of life. Theories, they feel, are almost irrelevant to the task of living. Concrete facts are life.

People are the world of the ESFP. All people-related jobs are transformed by the pleasure they bring. You can't help but love them, so if they choose public careers like the performing arts, fame and fortune may soon follow.

Some Areas for Growth

- Appreciation. Develop your appreciation for all others, not just for those with whom you agree.
- Reevaluation. Periodically revisit your values and ideas critically.
- Strengths. Develop your strengths and use them wisely.
- Centering on others. Living in the moment can become living for personal gratification; beware!
- Develop long range structure. Long-term vision will save the impulse of the moment from becoming all there is.
- Friendships. Make friends outside your comfort areas to help you grow.
- Intuition. Seek to intuit people's reasons for doing things and understand them more.
- Open-mindedness. See things from other people's point of view.
- Develop a disciplined life. Personal desire can take precedence over life's obligations, so become more aware of life's demands.
- Responses. Realize that the negative actions of people are not necessarily personal assaults.

- Personal growth. Keep developing the richness of your inner life.
- Develop your value system. Potential is reached not by sophistication, but by the development of inner values.

Stress for the ESFP

Feelings are the main cause of stress to the ESFP and the ISFP. SPs don't stress as much or for as long as the other temperaments, but when their feelings are disturbed, the stress button can be seriously pushed and stress can do its damage. Unhelpful reactions to the emotions that disturb their world can even make them aggressive.   Remember, emotions are the most powerful force in our brains and make such sudden protective reactions almost inevitable.

The disturbance typically comes when the ESFP finds that others do not react in ways they have planned or when they are convinced others should act. They have this optimistically pleasant way of feeling that others will think and react as they do. Most of the time people do, so we can hardly call it naive. When people don't, they stress over not knowing how to handle the situation in a way other than attacking the source of their disturbance.

We all get disturbed when our values are attacked or discounted, and the ESFP's values run deep. For them, one of those values to which they are very sensitive is personal freedom, which they can interpret with an absoluteness that realism can't support. We are only as free as others' rights, demands, and values will allow. Every member in a society conditions it and the personal freedom of each is conditioned likewise. Therefore, the ESFP's stress can often be reduced by a rational reappraisal of their value system.   They can consider that the responsibility and traditionalism of others are equal values to freedom.

A natural belief in their persuasive powers, and a conviction that what they choose as the right response to the present conditions is the only possible response, also lead to stress when these beliefs are challenged. Criticism is a case in point: It can wound, and wound deeply, anyone with an "F" in his or her profile. Much more so than the Ts, a serious attempt to criticize their values or the inner drives of their temperament will create internal stress.

ESFPs like to entertain, to live life on the lighthearted side, and to react freely to the demands of the moment. Therefore, an insistence upon behaving according to the serious, responsible traditions of the past can create a lot of stress for them.

Some people see life as a serious matter and regard the ESFP as flippant. Again, their values are being challenged at the root. The serious responsibilities of life and the matter-of-fact management of others can disturb the ESFP greatly.

ESFPs will make promises in the excitement of the moment that they can't keep and they load themselves with undesirable commitments. It's the bane of living with so much lighthearted optimism.

Stress is reduced by conditioning life with an understanding of all the values that others hold dear, not just a selective few, because most of the ESFP's stress arises out of disturbing relationships. Some structure to life; advice from wise, trusted friends, or an open-mindedness to what those that they perceive as their opposition believe, will greatly reduce their stress.

The Child

The developing ESFP struggles with all the factors of stress we have named, plus the lack of knowing which is the best response to a life they are still learning to understand. They do not know what the adult knows or, if they have been taught, they do not perceive things like an adult. Understanding others and their differences is perhaps the best thing to teach a young ESFP. Keep helping them understand and then hold them to making wise choices in all their relationships.

Freedom must be understood in order not to infringe on the freedoms of others. Freedom is felt by the freedom-loving ESFP as a right, not a privilege or even an earned right, and the difference is part of the parent's teaching agenda. Teach the privilege of freedom by requiring the honor of other people's freedom. Use reward as a motivational incentive, but the reward should always be earned; it should not be a gift.

Develop the skills and the individual talents (such as performing) of the ESFP, since this will make them feel you really understand who they are. An overly negative approach to this type will earn you a fast exit from their inner circle. You can't influence an ESFP who has excommunicated you.

These little children are enjoyable and a real pleasure, so keep the lightheartedness they crave a part of their home life, along with a little structure to teach them self-discipline. Boundaries are needed, of course, because a child can't know without more experience what is a wise boundary. Teach boundaries in a positive manner, not a negative one.

Overemphasize structure and you will get conflict for sure. An SJ parent must learn to treat the ESFP in the manner that they have been designed and not according to their own more serious temperament.

The Achilles Heel

To be unable to constructively take criticism can lead to a spiteful, bitter ESFP. Their feelings can, in this case, become bitter, and the pleasant, happy, entertaining ESFP becomes a disruptive force in relationships and a negative impact on themselves. They also become "anti-authority" — anyone's authority — and negatively attack all who oppose them and their perceived freedoms. This leads to an ESFP who displays all the opposite virtues of their type, except to the few that are still within their accepted circle. The ESFP has then transformed into the weaknesses of their flip side.

Summary

(This short summary can be a quick way of understanding the central themes of this type. Also, it can be used to check an assessment's accuracy by asking the person if they concur with a majority of these statements. Simply put, does it sound like them?)

ESFPs are performers and entertainers at heart. For them, all the world is a stage. The joy and excitement of living fills their hearts and guides their lives. This type truly lives optimistically for the moment. Their personal values are deep convictions within them, which they often express dramatically on behalf of themselves and others. How they present themselves is vital to their image and success.

They feel a great call to exercise their freedom and their rights, and in any cherished cause they are the most generous with their possessions, believing that this is a plentiful world and what they give away today will come back to them tomorrow.

These warm and affectionate performers love to work with people. They clown around and are naturally the center of attention. ESFPs will take risks. High-spirited, expressive, friendly, and warm, there is an irresistible charm about them. They take pleasure in stimulating others and when the rush of adrenaline subsides, they need stimulation too.

ISTP

Adventurous risk-takers, ISTPs are risk addicts, perhaps more than any other type, and find much of their fun in taking others on their enjoyable daring rides. Perhaps scaring them a little and finding out how much they can get away with seems to egg them on.

Speed, which all SPs enjoy, is a calling for most ISTPs. Not just being the fastest, but enjoying the **surges of adrenalin** and the **accolades** of onlookers motivates them too. They love **action** and all the stimulation it brings. Skiing, drag racing, motor cross, surfing, climbing, driving dune buggies, hunting, fishing, scuba diving, etc. — all are activities that can attract and test the deft judgment of this type. All things mechanical and technical attract them, and with their interest in crafting comes **a love of tools** and, for some, the thrill of controlling large equipment. Mechanical or technical things draw them, not just for the stimulation but, arousing their curiosity, it makes them want to know how and why they work the way they do.

Guns, weaponry, and the extremely skilled use of these deadly tools can soon make an ISTP salivate. The gunslingers of the Old West, with **lightning-fast responses** honed by months of rewarding practice, exemplify this type's interests. For them, practice does not carry the feeling of toil and long hours of pain; rather, all practice is living the experience in the mind repeatedly and feeling the appeal of speed and **tactical mastery**. Practice is exciting play.

Like the ESTP, their daring characterizes them and their **fearless spirit,** when activated, can draw them to such pursuits as specialty law enforcement squads, racing vehicles, and perhaps a career as a Navy Seal. For them, life is shortchanged if it does not **push the limits**. Injury will not dissuade them from facing danger again. All tools, from the delicate scalpel to the supersonic jet, and all technology, from the computer to the space vehicle, will excite them. It seems as though there is a secret pact between the ISTP and the world of things. That pact spells out adventure and excitement.

But danger is not the only attraction. Musical instruments or **the world of art** can make its case and lock them into its pleasures. Their **practical genius** and adeptness with all kinds of tools and instruments often leads them into the tech schools where they show their native artistry with anything that fits into their hands. They are the true masters of turning ideas into physically appealing results. Give them the general concept of what you want and they will retreat into the world of creativity and fashion it with deftness and appeal. An **impulsive creativity** lives in them, born of their native desire as SPs to be unfettered and free. They are also gifted with organizing abilities, showing a natural, **practical logic** that leads them to grasp the core of a problem.

Impulsive, with a mind that tactically seeks never to be outwitted by any circumstance, they respond with a belief in their quickness and skills that downplays the need for preparation. **Adaptable,** they can turn to almost anything in the physical world and excel.

Their introversion tends to make them distant, quiet, reserved, and **hard to get to know** until they feel at home with you. Unlike the ESFP, they are not typically talkative and this can make them less than involved in school and in class settings. They have, perhaps more often than other type, been labeled as dyslexic or slow at learning, which is most of the time just not true. Above all, they need learning to test their skills. They are not verbal creators, and this adds to the fact that the classroom atmosphere alienates them and bores them. Even though they are not necessarily book-smart, they are very smart when it comes to **street wisdom**. Their fast senses add to their skill in solving any immediate situation that confronts them.

Friends are those who love activity and admire the ISTP's giftedness with tools and machinery. ISTPs tend to isolate themselves from those with academic leanings, yet they are busy, skillfully analyzing what is happening around them with a detached curiosity. When they find a friend, they stick closer than a brother with a **generosity that is** second-to-none.

Communication mostly takes place with what they create and fashion and through their activities and actions. They would like to feel their **actions speak for them**. Because of a belief that this is a generous world and what we use today will be replaced tomorrow, they share warmly and with a light heart with their friends.

Flashes of original humor and the obvious **desire to impress** characterize an evening with them. But if you want to keep their friendship, don't try to restrict them or coddle them. Nor should you try to control them with a superior attitude or an authoritarian approach. They will simply be scarce but, if pushed too far, will show sudden bursts of anger.

They can be staunchly **insubordinate** and determinably lone rangers when they scent the hand of authority. Nothing, not even a deadline, will turn them from their interest and if the two clash, the deadline loses without guilt or conscience.

It's hard to raise these daredevils whose kindness overwhelms you and whose **waywardness** infuriates you. They live to leave home and be on their own, not because they dislike home but because something is calling. **The universe is calling,** making them want to learn to fly, ride their motorcycle in the rain, dance in the snow, surf with the sharks, explore outer space, walk on the moon, be "out there" (wherever "out there" is), and do as much as they can in the short life they, too, live.

Some Areas for Growth

- Flexibility. Learn to be flexible; not everyone wants your approach to their problem.
- Learning. Learn the way you learn best; hands on is the typical way.
- Refreshment. Guard your personal enjoyment of life and keep trying refreshing things.
- Enjoyment. Make your work fun and the environment in which you work stimulating.
- Motivation. Use your gifts and strengths to stay motivated.
- Depression. When feeling depressed, take time to enjoy what interests you.
- Organization. Set personal deadlines for making decisions.
- Emotions. Consider the emotions of other people more.
- Strategy. Develop a long-term frame of mind.
- Strengths. Increase your strengths.

Stress for the ISTP

The ISTP is little stressed by risk or challenge. In fact, it stimulates them. Personal failure and the boredom of working in a job that crushes their freedoms or allows no "in the moment" creativity are big stress factors. Stress will show itself in restlessness and a discontent, not only with the situation that caused the boredom, but with life itself. The ISTP will fidget around when there is no action, showing their distress. They need stimulation of mind and body to function happily. Activity alone can bring them out of their funk. Help them find activity and fun again in any of its forms. If no activity is possible, they love to regale you with stories of their adventures and come alive again when food, drink, and the opportunity to make an impression on others offer themselves.

They are skilled and fast with tools or equipment of any sort, and being made to feel that they must be taught by someone less skilled than they are will irritate and anger them. They will disrespect that person and build anxiety if forced to continue in this kind of environment. People of other temperaments who are not as gifted as they are at practical matters cause them tension and you are likely to see it.

Their patience also wears thin when having to watch others bungle their way through what the ISTP can do so easily and effectively. Incompetent workers or unskilled people annoy them. Respect and acceptance depends on showing competence and ability. If asked to instruct others they will do so, but they expect others to learn quickly. Often they will happily leave to others the task of teaching.

Failure eats away at their confidence and confidence is a product of their inherent optimism, so it breeds a significant loss of faith in them. Their introversion sends them inward when they fail, which is not where they want to live.

Feelings of failure are an emotion they seem not to be able to handle well. Failure also means that they have no opportunities to use their great skills or they are financially too limited to find opportunities. They are problem-solvers, and if the present moment has to be lived without any such opportunity, they soon become depressed. Among the SPs, the introverted ones (ISTP and ISFP) can become depressed more easily because of the inward nature of introversion.

Like most SPs, criticism is not taken well. They can explode in anger when criticized. They expect to succeed at everything they do, and they are their own worst critics. However, self-criticism spells failure to them in the most profound way and hence they fall under its pressures. Finding the chance to be the skilled workers and creators that they are is the best resolution to their stress. The optimism of their nature usually keeps them searching for these opportunities in the moment, but when stressed, even this leaves them.

The Child

Parents will often have to deal with the anger of failure. It can be an explosive moment but will soon pass if another chance to succeed is presented. Keep the young ISTP active and productive. See that they have the opportunity to show others their skills and feed off their abilities. ISTPs are made to succeed and every effort spent to help them achieve is an effort that avoids destructive behavior and mischief making.

They must be kept active. Teach them skills, but don't stand over them as though you doubt their ability to learn practical talents since that will provoke them. Let them show you their ability and correct only when necessary. They like to be the ones who show you their competence.

A less than optimistic attitude toward them will earn their disrespect. Positive parenting is the best approach, but not without the necessary teaching of boundaries and that adhering to those boundaries can make a person more productive and successful. Learn to show your pleasure and amazement at their successes and reward them for what they earn.

The Achilles Heel

Failure or a repeated forecast of failure is their Achilles heel. Take away the chance to show their skills or be creative with their hands and it is like chopping off their arms. They can't live in their minds alone; it seems like an incomplete world to them. The ISTP is built for a world of action, and in action they find their sense of purpose and their fulfillment.

Their finely tuned motor skills express who they are. Without a successful opportunity to express themselves, there is no fulfilled purpose in action and as the wilting of their strengths begins, they slide into a depression that feels more like uselessness than hopelessness. This depression leads in some to destructive behavior because there, at least, is the opportunity to make meaningful impact. Their self-image is built around making a successful impact, not on other values. Find with and for them a way to be who they are, and remove the obstacles that have derailed them.

Summary

(This short summary can be a quick way of understanding the central themes of this type. Also, it can be used to check an assessment's accuracy by asking the person if they concur with a majority of these statements. Simply put, does it sound like them?)

These great, practical problem-solvers, ISTPs, have a keen eye for how things work and the opportunities all things present. Skilled with tools and machines, from the jet fighter to the jackhammer and from computerized technology to the humble screwdriver, anything that requires masterful operation and a sharp, tactical mind seems to become an artistic device in their hands. Yes, and the real weapons too. The lightning-fast gunslingers of the Old West were most likely ISTPs.

ISTPs demand their independence and follow their hunches but not without a practical analytical evaluation of how things are likely to work. ISTPs can be fearless risk-takers and avid adventurers. Routine is boring; fun and games are stimulating; freedom is essential, and their crafting skills are second-to-none. ISTPs are impulsive, in-the-moment lovers of life, and masterful creators and crafters.

ISFP

A **muted** version of the SP, the ISFP surprises us a little by being so **retiring and quiet**. Under the smooth surface, however, the same desires beat and guide their lives as for all SPs. For example, the love of freedom that lives in the ISFP is still a strong driving force, but without the "in your face" push to have to be free.

An inbuilt desire to have their lives make an impact on others surges inside of them but it remains unnoticed. The same SP individualism, albeit not of a flashy and flamboyant variety, still pulls at them. Bravery, the badge of all SPs, makes them risk-takers too, but the daring spirit is kept on the inside and displays much more concern for the results of their actions. The **desire for fun** and for the enjoyment of life, supported by a still fierce optimism, remains the emotional powerhouse of the ISFP.

The ISFP is friendly, but in a more introverted manner than the ESFP. With their pleasant, warm, social demeanor comes **sensitivity** to others that is deep and kin to the ENFP's hypersensitivity. The difference is that the ISFP's sensitivity derives from their very finely tuned five physical senses rather than a super-active intuition. What does this look like? ISFPs sense the subtle nuances of life's adventures and reproduce them in a fine array of sensory expressions designed to entertain and stimulate our eyes, ears, taste buds, touch or smell. So the ISFP can produce or direct highly emotional works of art and creative masterpieces of all sorts. Their desire for fun plus the lightheartedness of their optimism also shapes their sensitivity.

As we have noted, they can excel in the world of composing, creative writing, the fine arts, commercial arts, the performing arts, and anything that stimulates the human senses. In this **world of the physical senses** they seem to know what suits the occasion with uncanny accuracy. In music and the fine arts, some have attained to becoming **virtuosos**. Keirsey calls them the composers, and not without reason.

Their expressive individualities will most likely be displayed in their creative work. Although they do write some compelling lyrics, in their day-to-day communications they display a disinterest in words as a means of communication and can even appear inexpressive.

They are more **modest** about their abilities than other SPs, though still showing a quiet confidence that comes from that underlying emotion of optimism. It gives them a reserved involvement with others that is rather appealing and invites a friendship. Disagreements don't mesh well with them and they will shun them, withdraw from them or occasionally show the anger that all of us can release when pushed too far.

They are **impulsive** and respond to the **instant inspiration**. The planning and preparation that went into their inspired moment did not come from the slavish hours others might have spent in perspiration and anxiety but the long years of practice, which to them is play and in which they fine-tune their skills and sensitivities. They seldom feel or regret the toil they endured gladly in the birth of their composition, work of art, design or, if they are chefs, their aromatic masterpieces.

Spontaneity can also be their source of inspiration in life or in their relationships. They can't wait to express their feelings with subdued confidence. All creativity must be driven by the moment of inspiration. Such suddenness captures them and they are carried along in its passion and sensory articulation.

Remember, they are **individualistic** so don't try to force your opinions on them. They form their own and they usually treasure an attitude of tolerance for others and their views. Forcing their own opinions down somebody's throat is not to their liking. If they feel someone is being too forceful and domineering of others they withdraw with inner distaste or even anger.

Seldom do they lead, but they follow people where they find reason to **establish loyalties** and like-mindedness. Being **reserved,** they are not the self-promoters that ESTPs are and can often be lost to the world in the silence of their lives. We will never know how many great compositions and works of art have been left unexposed to our world because of their disinclination to self-promotion. Passion to express their feelings and beliefs also lies under a thin veil of reserve.

Kindness is another word to describe them. While caring for others, especially the needy, they can suffer gladly, revealing their true philanthropic heart. They see the needy as the unfortunates, showing their anger at those who might suggest irresponsible behavior is the source of their wayward condition. "Be kind, not critical" is their mantra. In this, the NF, whose kindness and empathy is a native strength, is the only temperament to challenge their concern for others.

Speed is not necessarily a virtue to them. They believe in getting things done in a relaxed manner. The present moment can be spoiled with undue haste. Time itself is to be enjoyed.

It is easy to misunderstand this type and we sometimes type them wrongly as INFPs. And occasionally they are typed wrongly as ENFPs because their love of life and inherent optimism, along with their very sensitive nature, can make them seem to be NFs. A closer look will differentiate them.

Some Areas for Growth

- Experience. Open up to influences and experiences outside of your interests.
- Being overloaded means less time for impulsive inspirations, so live at your own pace.
- Communications. Where communication is essential, be verbal.
- Responsiveness. Remember, silence is not clear communication most of the time.
- Strengths. Live with quiet power in your strengths.
- Structure. Consider using a little structure to organize your talents.
- Decisiveness. Make decisions and don't let life make them for you.
- Details. Data and facts can enrich your personal judgments.
- Expressiveness. Passive resistance can backfire, so become more expressive.
- Focus on your strengths. Self-criticism can derail you.
- Self-esteem. When under-appreciated, find approval and praise; it is a need.
- Logic. Make room for the appreciation of logic.

Stress for the ISFP

A lack of recognition of their creative ideas and accomplishments can lead to much stress. Like all SPs, they need to make an impact, and when they don't it is a major area for their concern. First, when you see signs of stress, ask whether they are having success and receiving recognition for their success? Do they feel positive feedback? If not, give them your feedback and encourage them. Remind them that when the going gets tough the tough get going.

ISFPs like to focus undisturbed when at their creative activities. Disturbance of any sort will frustrate them. Stress occurs because they can't pursue the path their desires strongly urge them to take. It's the same SP problem of being confined or cabined. Freedom is gone for the moment and if this is persistent it will take the ISFP down.

Disturbances usually come in the form of people and those close to the ISFP, meaning these are the ones that will feel the results of stress in irritability and repressed or expressed anger. They must learn to include others in their world, if only as a token measure, while their creative juices flow. It amounts to a limiting of their sense of freedom for the sake of other goals precious to them.

All Ps, but especially this one, can become so engrossed with what they are doing that they forget deadlines and appointments and paying bills, making for stress upon stress until they cannot take the pressure. Time can become a burden rather than an opportunity. Some self-discipline is needed for them to be successful and stay connected to reality.

The other obvious cause of damaging stress for these intensely focused individuals is neglect of their personal needs and emotional burnout. Care must be taken to fuel and nurture their creative activities and that also means themselves. Simply asking them to relax and take it easy is not usually helpful since physical relaxation cuts off the flow of their inspirational juices. Better coping skills are learning to set goals that are realistic and to accept that the time goal may change so don't stress about it. They must learn to be upfront about their further needs. Ask for understanding and space to complete the task and always learn to keep communication flowing.

The Child

The child faces all the above problems, but with an added burden: the burden of not having a history of how to deal with the emotional pressures that their strengths and urges create. Emotional buildup that results from not handling the pressure can be an insurmountable stress. First, the child ISFP needs help, not negative criticism, when they fall under the weight of their emotions. Helping them find the way to handle their emotions is the goal of parenting in this case.

Without setting the expectations too high, they need to be helped to realize and accept the demands of life's realities and structure their lives somewhat to handle the requirements that will be placed on them. If taught while they are still young and very malleable, they can enter adulthood without feeling that the world is unfair and unduly harsh on them with its time constraints and demands.

You will notice that they don't seem to be always upfront about their need for freedom and activity like the other SPs, but look again. It is there, but in a muted form, and often they remain silent when frustrated. Careful observation helps the parent spot their needs and disturbance, and gentle intervention is then more a sign of the parent understanding than being too corrective or authoritarian.

Make sure to encourage and develop their strengths and especially to find the feedback they need to remain motivated. These are very sensitive children who need gentle, understanding parents who also maintain somewhat flexible boundaries to help the child adjust to reality.

The Achilles Heel

Criticism and a lack of feedback can bring them down fast. They must learn to handle criticism of their work. Otherwise they will keep folding rather than persisting to be all they can be. All sensitive types will need to be able to disconnect from the negative and connect to the positive.

Tools to accomplish this task are: distraction (when needed) from the criticism of others, the ability to remain focused on their goals and on the positive feedback, reason to sort out what is not valid criticism and what is helpful and constructive, and a self-image that can weather the heat of other people's lack of insight. These and anything that helps them keep themselves above the negative will strengthen them and make them more creative and productive.

Summary

(This short summary can be a quick way of understanding the central themes of this type. Also, it can be used to check an assessment's accuracy by asking the person if they concur with a majority of these statements. Simply put, does it sound like them?)

Being sharply attuned to all that goes on around them and the feelings that move the hearts and minds of people, ISFPs are amazing composers and directors of any art form if given the opportunity. They are also sensitive and skilled at interpreting what their five senses tell them, resulting in sensory masterpieces created on the palettes of their minds. Relationships, if the ISFP is allowed room to express himself, can be skillfully woven expressions of love as well. Being feelers of life's heartbeats and both sympathetic and loyal, they live and love according to the drummer in their own hearts.

They are not self-promoters and the world sees little of what many of them can achieve. Reserved and quiet, they say little, preferring to publish their thoughts through the eloquent medium of what they do and keeping the rest to themselves. Even when some of them become famous they are still reserved and hidden souls. Their work is the result of inspiration and spontaneous impulses rather than the labor of preparation and planning. Friendly, warm, optimistic, and kind, they are the more subdued playmates and live absorbed in their inspirations.

The SJ Temperament

ESTJ

ESTJs are the **natural supervisors,** seeing to it that everything functions smoothly. But supervision also implies a willingness and natural need to **control** all things including people. They do not hesitate. ESTJs feel bad if they don't see to it that others, not just themselves, **obey the rules**.

Being extroverts, they focus their control on people by means of systems. Being Ss, they are in the moment and no one can escape their supervision for long. They even feel obligated to report offenders for the good of everyone else. All SJs have a penchant and a need for controlling life, and ESTJs lead the way. When things are out of control, their foundation quakes and they become unstable, looking for security of some sort: anything to return a sense of solidity to life. Authority is respected by supervisors and, even as children, they model a respect for those in charge.

ESTJs feverishly keep lists, schedules, and inventories, all with the purpose of knowing where they are in relation to their goals and what needs attention. A supervisor can't operate effectively without **routines, systems, rules, and regulations**. ESTJs depend on their systems and are highly defensive of the rules and regulations. In fact, they will often create regulations to protect regulations; such is their **passion for order**. They fashion them in true linear fashion and operate them with a divine dictum.

Family life is conducted in the same responsible model. Home life is to run efficiently and woe betide the child who does not knuckle down to the systems the ESTJ has confidently put in place. They do not hesitate to discipline and feel no sympathy for the offender either.

Respect is demanded and rarely seen as something that also must be earned. Along with it, **good manners** are expected. The tried and true ways at home and at work are trusted. **Traditions** are honored and all, including the spouse, should keep their feet firmly planted in the past and in its proven ways of doing things. **Celebrations and social**

fraternizing are welcome activities that keep the connection to the past healthy.

Don't try to fix something that is not broken. And never ask who is the leader; the ESTJ assumes the role without appointment and controls the life of the group, **giving orders** as deemed necessary. They bark out demands with a natural ease. Demanding and, at times, judgmental of those under them, they are cooperative with those over them, honoring rank and status in the accepted **chain of command**.

Insecurity is their Achilles heel, so we need to say more about it. The stable nature of their temperament collapses and displays the opposite when security is lacking in their lives. In the child ESTJ, undesirable behavior will quickly result when the child is insecure. The adult is no less susceptible to such bouts of anxiety and breakdown. In particular, the ESTJ will show this insecurity by battening down the hatches and preparing for the worst. To others, this appears to be **stubbornness,** while it is really the expression of fears that are attacking the security of their core. This can lead to insubordination in a business setting and to dismissal when, in fact, the problem can be solved if the cause of their insecurity is removed.

If anything, the ESTJ is **practical** and wants to live in the world of reality. The real world, as opposed to the world of fantasy and imagination, is where they make their home. Down-to-earth, reliable, and putting up with no nonsense describes them well.

With this passionate **realism** comes a seriousness that sets them apart from all the SPs. Life is serious business and everyone must show they understand this or invite the ESTJ's dislike. A strong sense of responsibility follows, and that means personal responsibility for all we do and all the choices we make. **Conscientious** to the core and hard working, their seriousness is cuffed to realism and duty. If a job has to be done, those who daydream or fool around wasting precious time are castigated. Such irresponsible nonsense will not be tolerated.

Matter-of-factness follows. Facts are their basis for a matter-of-fact attitude. To the ESTJ, facts are what is known and proven by experience and what is devoid of emotional trauma. Therefore, a relationship that is emotionally charged can be a real challenge to them. Unfamiliarity with emotions leads them to supervise their loved ones **by the book**.

Change bothers them. Change opens the door to insecurity because they don't know how a new procedure will work out. Will it fail or introduce a new tradition? The anxiety such waiting and worrying produces is often too much to handle for the ESTJ. Therefore, theories, which are uncertainties until proven that they work, are also suspect. Theories live in the unreal world of possibilities and threaten the belief that only what is proven and tested is worthy of application. It's the fear of the threat that unnerves them most. Imagination is for children. Adults grow out of it and plant their feet on terra firma. Always, ESTJs must have a stable footing. And when they do, they appear as **solid** as the rock of Gibraltar.

Even though change is an issue for them, they have a good **head for business** because they will instinctively create systems and routines to keep change at a measured pace, and then supervise and manage change with their systems. **Organization** comes naturally to them but if they are disturbed by insecurity they plunge into a state of disorganization. When needing to learn something new, they function best when they can immediately apply what they have learned.

Decisive and quick to put their decisions into operation, they also take care of the details of the implementation. Details, even lots of them, don't create panic for the ESTJ — rather a challenge to show their metal. With these abilities, they often rise quickly to become **administrators as well as supervisors**.

Community is important to them and their supervisory abilities, combined with strengths of reliability, responsibility, and trustworthiness, make them the **cornerstones of institutional and civic life**. They may gravitate to organizations such as churches, clubs, civic committees, school committees, and lodges because of their skills and their need to belong and to find **social engagement**. **Leadership** follows.

Some Areas for Growth

- Refrain from overuse and misuse of supervision that amounts to controlling others against their will.
- Avoid over-decisiveness; take time to think through your decisions carefully.

- Learn to manage change so that you do not break down into worry.
- Become less rigid in enforcing regulations.
- Temper your determination by not digging in your toes and refusing to bend.
- Exhibit patience when enforcing details.
- Make decisions with consideration for the views of others rather than forcing decisions based on your interpretation of the facts.
- Attend to the needs of others in a relationship.
- Avoid criticizing others who do not share the same convictions.
- Realize that change is a constant and learn to manage and welcome its benefits.
- Honor the privacy of introverts.
- Faith. When worry settles on you, work on trust and faith.
- Strengths. Live in wise control of your strengths.
- Flexibility. Know that exceptions are not necessarily a breach of the rules.
- Realize the importance of following the *spirit* of the regulation as well as the letter of the rule.
- Light heartedness. Lighten up a little.

Stress for the ESTJ

When people are not cooperative and thwart the plans of an ESTJ, they can feel great stress. They so firmly believe in their systems and plans and all the policies and procedures that accompany them that they cannot imagine others not jumping aboard and working consistently as programmed. Besides, all these things are the way to the common goals of a company or a group, and how could anyone not want to efficiently do what the goals demand? Frustration and fear that the goal will not be reached can keep them awake at night and fill their day with greater determination to see to it that all is done according to plan.

The response of an ESTJ to the frustrations of people management is often anger, whether outwardly expressed or inwardly contained, and being such driven and demanding personalities they do themselves great harm. Anger eats away at the health of their bodies, and they can often neglect their own health needs in the panic of having to achieve efficiency and success.

Their own drives can cause them further stress. The need for them to be responsible (and that means everyone under them to be responsible) and the demand for reliability and consistency, along with a determination to be right, are ingredients in the SJ's stress profile. Worry can set in quickly and be defended as the only way to exhibit responsibility, and that makes them even more stress prone.

Depression is often avoided by an active form of worry, which demands increasing effort be expended on the avoidance of failure. Self-doubt and the feeling of uselessness are then skirted in the urgency of fixing the problem.

The simple lack of progress is an early flag and can plunge the ESTJ into a whirlwind of activity designed to force progress. "If things are going wrong apply more pressure" is their solution and a recipe for increased stress with all of its ugly results. Inefficient use of time, waste in any form, loss on the bottom line, causes a rise in inner tension that can be explosive.

Stress can be reduced when the ESTJ accepts human error and writes it in as part of the plan. Time markers can be changed and kept somewhat flexible so that achievement is within parameters rather than measured by an unbendable mark of progress. They must learn not to take the frustrations of the job home or to take the upsets caused by one party and infuse them into the more delicate relationships of family and friends. Setting more realistic goals for children who do not yet have the experience and mental and emotional development expected of adults can reduce stress further.

They must seriously deal with the demon of worry and learn how to control its damaging emotions. They shouldn't take the entire responsibility; sharing it with others is an essential people skill. They should find really relaxing recreations and never take their worries with them when they play. They will learn that life is not only work; it is play as well.

The Child

For the child, all the above stresses as infants can be largely offset with the right parenting. Applying pressure to make an ESTJ child obey is effective at times, but will eventually prevent him from learning to reign in his own tendencies. Teaching them to reason and helping them achieve an image of always being logical and reasonable rather than emotionally highjacked is where the greatest parenting effort is needed.

When the child tries to make other children obey and be responsible, the parent can help him understand that we do not fight the battles we can't win but only those we can. Training him to understand that a little honey is more effective than an angry demand is good. Teaching good people skills will set him up for a great future of becoming a manager of others.

Showing the child how little anger can achieve and how much he can gain from tact and people skills is essential on the parenting agenda too. He must know how to ask for assistance and how to forgive and forget since he, too, is imperfect and in need of the same.

The Achilles Heel

The Achilles heel for the ESTJs is the insecurity of being unable to control their environment and what their success engenders. This boils down to the inability to control others. When things are out of control and they can't follow their plans or those of their superiors, they hit the panic button. All that achieves is what the button says: panic. Order sometimes goes out the door along with reasonable behavior, and the world of the ESTJ crumbles.

They are known for their stability in times of pressure, and when the opposite is the result of insecurity, they begin to fall completely apart. Unfortunately for many, they then do the only thing they know to do: they apply more force and try to control all the more. At this point they become leaders without a following and depression can now set in.

The ESTJs are in need of people skills and an understanding of successful methods other than rules, regulations, and authoritarian demands. Taught this, they become their best and are unsurpassed as leaders and supervisors of projects.

Summary

(This short summary can be a quick way of understanding the central themes of this type. Also, it can be used to check an assessment's accuracy by asking the person if they concur with a majority of these statements. Simply put: Does it sound like them?)

ESTJs are gifted organizers and excel in producing structure and consistency. Chaos is the evil demon, and planning and supervision are the angels of progress. They mostly see life as work and they live to work rather than work to live. Industrious, conscientious, and dependable, ESTJs supervise others and, as a result, make the world go round. They liberally hand out approval if performance has earned it but, if not, the contractual agreement is immediately revoked.

Rules, regulations, and agreements must not be messed with. These responsible stalwarts of organization know that people must follow the rule or that demon of chaos rises to ruin everything. Consequences are part of management and ESTJs even feel obligated to call anyone to account for their infringements in order to enforce the rules. How can anyone imagine society can flourish any other way? They save for a rainy day but, like the grasshopper in the *Ant and the Grasshopper*, if someone comes knocking in need, they open up their stored goods and their heart. ESTJs are realists, good mannered, and cooperative administrators whose love of work is only challenged by their love of home, family, and tradition.

ESFJ

These are **warm, friendly, personable** types. They exude a caring loving attitude, giving happily of themselves to others. Because they wish to provide for the **material welfare** of others, they are constantly on the lookout for the needs of others. Furnishing what people need, serving their wants, catering to their every desire, they set themselves up for being seen as the quintessential **host or hostess**, the world's caterers. Keirsey has rightly named their outward orientation as "Providers."

ESFJs soften the image of SJs in general. They are **a little less serious,** although they are given to worry and anxiety when the pressure is on, turning negative at times. Even then, they surface as **caring providers,** seeking solutions to their concerns and not simply wallowing in their hurt.

The warmth I mentioned in some ESFJs is sincere and they hurt when rebuffed or disrespected almost as much as an NF. Those with a strong feeling function appear tender too. Although still all about justice and fairness, they **lean toward mercy** and often will respond opposite to the STJs on this issue. Consideration for others' circumstances and their sad plight in life touches their hearts more readily.

Talkative, even more so than the ESTJ, conversation is an outlet for their tensions and a natural platform for their social lives. Getting together to talk about their friends and their fortunes or misfortunes can energize them easily. "Thank God," they say, "for texting, phones, Skype, and all social media." As a result they are **popular,** with pleasant, outgoing personalities. No one is a stranger and they make friends with a naturalness that is rewarding to all.

Their sympathy (the Greek word indicates that it is *standing alongside of others in their suffering*) is genuine and they are perhaps the most **sympathetic** of all the types, contributing to their universal appeal. This fascination with other people's concerns can cause them to become mildly to severely depressed at times. They quickly attract attention in a group and monopolize the news or the **gossip**. In fact, they are the local social newspaper!

Bent on doing their duty and being responsible, they are (like all SJs) **conscientious,** and among the SJs they are the most **cooperative**. Being team workers, they are not happy working alone for long periods of time. **Seldom are they seen working alone** at any project. Their ability at keeping people working together and focused on the purpose of the team is legendary.

Committees appeal to them, since they provide a social occasion and an opportunity to serve and accommodate the needs of others all in one assignment. And if the committee needs **leadership** and organizational skills to prepare for a convention, seminar or fundraiser, they will offer and complete the task with excitement, a sharp eye to detail, and excellence.

They will also take to the platform and perform the "Master of Ceremonies" role with distinction. Public speaking of this sort does not seem to faze them. Not only do they serve with distinction, but they have the knack for co-opting others to help them. When organizing an occasion, the ESFJ will provide well for everyone and make them feel important in an unassuming manner that sets everyone at ease. These loving, organizational feelers and providers often lead organizations and clubs.

But all this willing service and care for people's needs comes with a demand for **harmony.** Sensitivity to others and their feelings, which is how they are gifted, does not preclude an equal sensitivity to their own emotional needs. All who have a strong "F" function find themselves insisting on harmony and respect for their own feelings.

Disharmony is the opposite condition and, for a provider, does not allow them to function effectively. It is the negative spirit, not so much the fairness or unfairness of the squabble, that upsets them so. It is hard for an ESFJ to cater to the needs of those who are constantly fighting. So, ESFJs go all out to create a happy, positive atmosphere for family and friends, even while feeling drained themselves. This love and care for others demands love and care in return. Neglect loving them and you will pay by the loss of their greatest asset.

When pushed too far they can erupt in anger that is all the more effective because it is so surprising. They are not afraid of speaking up for themselves and, in true SJ fashion, arguing for their own point of view. **Emotions** are important to them. If you show a lack of feeling and concern for others you will be in the direct line of their disdainful fire.

ESFJs are made to be **home providers**. All the needs of the home plus the organization they feel it needs is meticulously taken care of. If the home of an ESFJ is not cared for, it is because the occupants have been abused them to the extent that they have become demotivated — a serious condition and one that needs rectifying before chronic depression takes over.

In the world of commerce, they make great **service people** or even **sales people,** personalizing all their arguments with an integrity that shows their genuineness. The customer is truly the king and they will bend the rules to accommodate the need of treating others with the respect they feel they deserve. The company is still honored, in their estimation. All who they deal with will be shown a **loyalty** that makes them great personal supporters. Their family and children are treated to the same supportive and loyal commitment.

Because they are always trying to do something nice for someone, their need for encouragement can be overlooked. It is a serious need. Without adequate **encouragement and praise,** they can quickly sink into negativity and aberrant behavior. When under-appreciated, the wrath of an ESFJ can produce a verbal broadside often followed by a return of the ice age, warning all of their disrespectful behavior. Providing for others will continue though, even if they are disrespected, but the atmosphere is negatively charged.

All this means the ESFJ is fascinated with people and their lives and focuses on whatever directly affects the lives of others. Being SJs, they also take values, responsibility, order, and being acceptable in society's eyes, seriously.

Some Areas for Growth

• Learn to deal positively with insecurity in relationships.

- Discover how to overcome discouragement from a lack of encouragement and praise.
- Develop skills at making decisions when people's feelings oppose your suggested course of action.
- Resist falling into worry and negativity when insecurity strikes.
- Overcome self-doubt in the face of a controlling figure.
- Live in the confidence that using your strengths will bring fulfillment.
- Develop the ability to deal with the truth about trusted and respected people.
- Overcome the tendency to let an authority rule when the actions of the authority are questionable.
- Discover true forgiveness to avoid getting hurt easily and holding a grudge.
- Emotions. Try not to understand everyone's emotions. Emotions are complicated.
- Letting go. On occasions, let people struggle so they can grow.
- Independence. Learn that independence is not an evil.
- Realize that it's okay to say "no."
- Learn that using control is not a good method to force peace and harmony.
- Respect that not everyone loves tradition and the standards of the past.
- Solve issues by returning good for evil rather than evil for evil.
- Optimism. Foster courage and a little optimism.

Stress For the ESFJ

The connections with home, family, and the community are the focal point of ESFJs' lives. Therefore, stress in these areas can unbalance them and does so quickly. Although they are all about keeping the rules in these communities, the breaking of the rules not only causes concern that the goal is not achieved for the smooth functioning of the community, but also for the harmony of the relationships that have been disturbed. When both the orderly functioning of the community and the harmony among its individuals has broken down, the ESFJ finds it hard to function. Then, they run out of ways to deal with the situations and begin the downward cycle into despair. Stress has taken its toll.

Overload is a common cause of stress in ESFJs. They want to help everyone all the time, which is an unrealistic urge that has to be disciplined if they are to manage their stress. To deal with this stress, they must first steady their emotions. Nervous emotions are a result of their stress. Calm and peace, trust, and faith are the elements that make for a stable SJ. They must use loving methods, not forceful methods, with understanding and an attempt to bond if they are to be successful in creating peace and a solid base to their community.

Approval is even more important for the ESFJ than the ESTJ; the need for harmony in a group is the reason. The ESFJ wants to know, "Am I doing my job well and am I connecting with everyone effectively?" A lack of approval is a prime cause for stress that builds quite dramatically and is usually not disclosed to even those who are close. If the ESFJ does not get involved with helping others they have no feedback of their place in the society, which is another cause of their stress.

ESFJs can turn critical and judgmental when people do not follow the expectations and rules of a group, and they then appear the opposite of their warm, friendly selves. The worry and negativism create guilt and self-dislike, which mutates quickly into depression. The judgmental attitude only destroys the best of their relationships and robs them of being asked to help. The cycle of destruction can then become vicious.

To reduce stress, they should first live in their strengths and be who they are, focusing on the positive instead of the hurtful negatives. They should also forgive readily without recalling the offense; they should try to forget it. They must look at people without their history infecting the mind. They will benefit from a return to warmth, love, and a friendship that shows constant interest in the needs and interests of others.

ESFJ's should not overload themselves with helping others or they will self-destruct. They need to see the importance of letting people help themselves and learn to recognize when they must withdraw and leave others to their own resources. Most of their stress is centered on the desire to help and the need for security.

The Child

The child will be a helpmate, but lack of approval will cause all kinds of unexpected behavior. The need for approval in an ESFJ shows up early. Make sure he or she is feeling appreciated. As a parent, you will need to ask how your child feels because he is not likely to communicate his need.

As he ages he can become too involved in activities and groups and in leadership of organizations. This spells overload. He will offer to help whenever and wherever the occasion to be of service arises. Monitor this willingness and teach him early the need to keep all things in balance.

He should be cooperative and helpful; if not, something is wrong. Act quickly and find out what it is that makes him do what he does if his behavior is destructive. Erratic behavior is always the clue to something that is amiss.

Loyalties will develop and he will not want to squeal on his friends. Worry about relationships is a main cause of stress. ESFJs will need, at times, to be more assertive. Also, they will need help in taking care of their own needs rather than the needs of their friends since others can come first for the ESFJ for many reasons.

The Achilles Heel

Overload leads to things not being done, resulting in guilt. If there is a breakdown of the ESFJ's personal community, it will quickly create insecurity, which is stress at its worst for them. Overload also causes health issues and when overtaxed, a bitterness and anger toward others and the world destroys all that is good and loving about the ESFJ.

The discipline of self-management must be learned to keep them functioning in their strengths.

Summary

(This short summary can be a quick way of understanding the central themes of this type. Also, it can be used to check an assessment's accuracy by asking the person if

they concur with a majority of these statements.   Simply put, does it sound like them?)

ESFJs show their feelings in a warm, caring smile and an obvious acceptance of you. They exude a willingness to meet your needs and are the world's great hosts and hostesses. Because they must care, they listen and sympathize. If it is at all possible, and even if it is not possible, they will attempt to accommodate everyone and meet their divergent needs.

They will charm you with their talents, admiring other people's success, always trying to keep things pleasant, and showing their gift of remembering names. These providers of people's needs are focused on people's welfare and care, but in turn, need people to recharge their generously spent energies.

ESFJs take care of details, are generous with their time, are nostalgic and sentimental in their conversations (they love to talk), and insist on traditional values. However, they are not all sweetness and hospitality. They will hold people accountable and show their disdain for irresponsible behavior. Society must be nurtured and controlled, hence their social contribution is two-sided. ESFJs show all the strengths of the SJs, but with a softer touch.

ISTJ

There are many admirable things about this type, although few give them due praise. The ISTJ is **loyal** to a fault. Treat them with respect; that is all they ask, and they will give you their devotion. Fail to do this and they will stand their safe distance, withdrawing into themselves without thinking of the consequences. When appreciated, they will turn in their grave for you.

Super dependable, the ISTJ is a standout performer. Loyalty and super-dependability compete in them with a **dedication to duty** second to none. They whip themselves if ever they are caught at being less than these things. With these traits you might expect a remarkable ability to focus, and it shows in a resolute determination in all they do. ISTJs are **socially pleasant** but not the center of attraction, preferring to abdicate attention for being the dependable people that they are and the **guardians** of all that is legal, moral, right, and fair.

However, all the above is negated when they are not appreciated, approved for their voluminous contribution of unstinting service, and adequately respected. They desire love and insist on appreciation.

All success must be earned by intense **concentration** and **thoroughness**. So exhaustive is their concentration that they pay no attention to protests or distractions. Things must wait until they have found a time when their concentration can relax. "Full steam ahead" is the order from their inner helmsman. The belief that concentration and thoroughness lead to success drives their core emotions, too, and is not only vigorously applied to themselves, but they will readily comment on the slackers and the lazy with emotional disdain. ISTJs believe everyone should pull their weight. Their feet are solidly planted in a **practical world** where they are always, if anything, **decisive**.

They worship **order** of their own sort but, when overwhelmed with their self-appointed goals, they can sometimes let orderliness slide for the time being. "Everything in its appointed place" is a dictum those who live with an ISTJ are well-advised to honor.

A **matter-of-fact** attitude to life is typical of them and it is driven by a **logistical**, linear mind that seeks to control their world with enforced consistency. You are part of their world and expected to conform to their expectations of logic.

Step-by-step procedures and **detailed investigation** of your ideas is the norm for these logicians. Because of this, they can make excellent teachers unless confronted with global minds who don't think logistically.

The ISTJ is perhaps the most **serious** of the SJs, which is saying something. Their seriousness is centered on their adherence to the **rules and regulations**. Not only do they seriously police themselves, but they feel no conscience about making certain the infringements of others are treated seriously too. In this they are like the ESTJ.

Rules cannot be broken. If the rule is there, it is the rule, and why would anyone think for a moment that the rule should not be enforced? Someone has to do the dirty work, and they are patient in their vigilance. Everyone should follow the procedures and rules and adhere to the standards, and that brings us to "Why should anyone expect not to be held **responsible** for his actions?" Hard-nosed about holding people accountable is a phrase often used of them. They are falsely seen as having no heart. It is not that the ISTJ only wants to hold everyone else accountable; they will submit willingly to their own standards. However, they cannot accept any avoidance of this divine commonsense law of life.

If breaking the rule seems wise (a difficult admission for an ISTJ), another rule is needed to replace it. ISTJs are patient with procedures and rules but not always patient with others, although they feel they seldom show their impatience.

We should note: they are easily offended and open to the hurts of criticism, which is hard to remember when they can seem so stern and unapproachable. Of the SJs they are the least appreciated. They do not earn this insult. They are also the most complicated of the SJs because of their hidden responses and non-communication.

Therefore, regardless of opinions, they are the serious **inspectors**. If responsible for products or setup, nothing escapes their fierce scrutiny.

The dictionary says to inspect is to look at others closely to discover any shortcomings. "What good is done if an infringement is overlooked?" they ask.

Once others feel the reality of this characteristic, the ISTJ earns another dislike. The enforcer of the law, the inspector, never wins a popularity contest and this type may wonder why, because they are quite sociable and can be impressively pleasant. It is hard to live with such dislike or to see the title "inspector" as a strength, but it is. Our society would crumble without the vigilance of ISTJs.

Lying is hypocritical to realists and they are the **ultimate realists,** finding it hard to appreciate or function in a world of make-believe, dreams, and fantasy, except if that world is the world of a child.

They are also fiercely **independent**. If things go wrong, the ISTJ will set their jaw and tough it out or find a way around the event. They must make up their own minds about what needs to be done. Inspectors, of necessity, do this. Judgments must be made and the need for **being right** weighs as a serious pressure on their minds.

One thing leads to another and for every effect, there is a cause. If the child disobeys an order, the ISTJs believe a rebellious heart is the cause. The world of **cause and effect** is reality to them and it contributes to their understanding of logistical thought. No type is more insistent on the essential nature of **responsible behavior** and the need for consequences for those who infringe. The legal system, to which they can be attracted, is based on the understanding of cause and effect. All the other characteristics of SJs apply equally to the ISTJ, such as traditional, a protector of ceremonies, law abiding, stable, and stoical with a solid work ethic that can earn them the judgment of being workaholics.

Quietness and a reputation for being the most **non-communicative** of the types makes life, at times, for the ISTJ a negative experience and engenders criticism. This lack of communication creates the very real possibility of being misunderstood. They tend to keep to themselves as a result. Feelings are internalized and opinions are held close to the chest. If the ISTJ is not struggling to be of service to their loved ones something is drastically wrong.

Some Areas for Growth

- Factor the emotions of other people into your actions and decisions.
- It is beneficial to cultivate intimate relationships.
- Personal care. You have a need to take care of yourself and your time.
- Take care not to let logistical procedures overlook the feelings of others.
- Control the tendency to become a workaholic.
- Strengths. You are attractive because of your strengths; develop them and don't focus on your weaknesses.
- Avoid inspecting the actions of others to the point of controlling them.
- Overcome your need to always go by the book and exercise no leeway when the book does not cover all contingencies.
- Refrain from becoming judgmental of others
- Become less free with your inspective criticism.
- Learn to delegate when the load is too much to handle.
- Learn to take small risks with measured optimism.
- Flexibility. Let people do things their own way or they may walk
- Begin to see the bigger picture and its effects on current decisions rather than just seeing the next detail
- Recreation. Find people who get you away from work and out in the world to have fun
- Communication. Practice verbal communication to reduce being misunderstood

Stress for the ISTJ

Stress can be a constant factor for ISTJs. They are always policing the world because they feel the need to do so and demand to do their part in protecting against chaos. This means the stress of constant vigilance, even more so than the ESTJ, builds taxing tensions. But they also police themselves with a vengeance at times. Some will lower their personal stress by lowering the standards for themselves, but this is not a true example of the strongly ethical ISTJ.

When stressed by their own failures, they will act like stoics, blaming themselves, showing little if any emotion, and telling no one. Guilt churns within and they choose to simply batten down the hatches and prepare to face the consequences of their actions, rather than sharing their failure and seeking solutions. They will be the first to try to fix the problem for other people who are in stress, which seems to contradict their personal behavior.

They load each day with more than can be achieved and often go to bed with a vague sense of failure. Because this is constant, some means of handling the pressures has to be worked out. They will typically choose to lower the stress by working harder or longer, ignoring the signs of breakdown or fatigue and wearing themselves out with the demand to get all of their agenda completed. Inevitable irritability, plus ignoring the needs of others close to them in order to get the jobs done will cause even more stress. Because of this overload of stress, some will settle for a lesser standard and just get used to it. It results in a "don't care" or lethargic attitude and they then slide into a compromise with their conscience. What bring relief are the constant distractions of things that should be done, whether related or unrelated to their immediate task. These things become an immediate necessity to them, breaking their focus and causing a scattered center of interest.

If they are unable to fix a broken relationship or some major problem, stress can overwhelm them. They are made to be fixers of problems, and the inability to do anything constructive can cause them to dissolve and meltdown.

They need to know what is expected of them. If the instructions are vague, they falter in their performance and the uncertainty makes them feel insecure. Uncertainty then shakes their world. They will react with a defense of their needs and behavior, increasing their own tension whenever their superiors or partners keep changing things. Their mantra is "rules are rules" and you stick with them in order to avoid stress.

When the ISTJ has labored without thanks or approval they can turn negative and resentful with yet another stress afflicting them. They never feel they have earned a rest or a play date until others force the issue. An ISTJ should schedule play and pampering and learn to treat it as just another duty they must perform to be the best that they can be.

The Child

Although we would not choose the word "delicate" to describe this child, he is in need of special care when young. Hammering the need for a solid work ethic only causes him to grow up with an understanding of duty that is interpreted as an overuse of responsibility. He often forgets to be responsible to himself and needs to be taught self-care. Play is to be stressed for the little ISTJ. Enjoyment must be seen as a need, not only a reward for labor and conscientiousness. Weaknesses are usually an overuse of his strengths.

This child lives with determination, teeth gritted in a doggedness to do what he feels he has to do and not so much on the uplifting feelings that a good self-image brings. Hence, even when his self-image is low, he keeps performing while others don't or find they can't. What he has to do is sometimes what he wants to do and he can apply the same determination to "want-to's" as he does to "have-to's."

You see only the tip of the iceberg with this child and what you don't know needs to be discovered in those private personal talks that penetrate his reserve. If, as a parent, you see increasing introversion and withdrawal, something is probably happening unseen to you and it is a flag to go on a search for the troubling issue. Likewise, if disobedient and destructive behavior shows itself, his flag is waving and something is deeply affecting him.

This child cannot get enough approval and love, so make him feel important, especially if there is an extroverted child in the family. Keep him living in his strengths and let him earn all he is willing to, since this will make him into a highly productive and needed adult.

The Achilles Heel

Insecurity again surfaces as the Achilles heel of all SJs. However, in the ISTJs it shows itself in the uncertainty of change, ambiguously defined responsibilities, and in the lack of positive and affirming feedback. They are determined and want their formidability to be exercised within the rules and approved for its faithfulness.

Being anything less than responsible, reliable rule keepers is not enough for them. If there is no stated rule, expect that they will perform to their own rules. When you challenge their own rules, you directly challenge their logical conclusions as well as their sense of responsibility and, therefore, you can expect the confrontation to turn into a downward spiral.

The way out of uncertainty is certainty and approval. For them, it is to confront the source of change and uncertainty and find out what has to be done. They must clarify the rules. Put this powerful ISTJ train back on the tracks and the problem of insecurity has been largely solved.

Summary

(This short summary can be a quick way of understanding the central themes of this type. Also, it can be used to check an assessment's accuracy by asking the person if they concur with a majority of these statements. Simply put, does it sound like them?)

Doing their duty with all seriousness is the hallmark of the ISTJ. Work must come first but play should not be lost in their intense sense of responsibility. They are the logistical masterminds, sequencing and planning with remarkable skill.

They are super-dependable, traditional, conservative in dress and philosophy, and stable and conscientious in all they do. Loyalty to their commitments, their roles, and their loved ones is only matched by their need to do the right thing and develop all the good qualities that their culture demands of them. A stiff upper lip is the true stoic way an ISTJ faces adversity, grinding their way through whatever confronts them.

These are the inspectors of systems, routines, performance, and of people in any role. Nothing gets by the sharp observance of an ISTJ. Strictness is applied to all, especially themselves. They will not abide their own failures, coming down hard on themselves. When insecure or when not receiving positive feedback and approval, they can fall apart.

ISTJs can be withdrawn and remote if they feel unappreciated or overwhelmed. They desire love and show it liberally in all they do for others, which is appreciation they need. Socially, they are pleasant and can be charming, and when happy, their seriousness subsides and their warmth shines.

ISFJ

A glance at these letters will suggest that the ISFJ is a kind of cross between the ISTJ and the ESFJ. This does not make them any less unique or distinct as a type. They are **quiet,** with a **seriousness** that resembles the ISTJ. They are **friendly** and **very social** but more **reserved** about it than the ESFJ. This shyness can be mistaken as coldness or stiffness and suggests to some the appearance of an aloofness or disconnectedness. If any type is sincere this one is, with an honest sympathy that warms their sincerity.

Being **responsible** is very important to them and they want others to be held accountable to their promises too. Very often their major concern is the **downtrodden in society** and the formation of adequate laws to protect them from any unfair treatment. However, their concern for others does not end with protecting the poor; they are bent on **protecting the rights and needs** of all others, much like the ESFJ provides for the needs of all others. People need protecting, they believe. Their protection in terms of the **safety and security** of others can be fierce if they think that those who can't (in their view) fend for themselves are being neglected or being unfairly taken advantage of.

Their weapons of choice are the **rules and regulations** they can successfully impose and, like all SJs, they will work diligently on committees and boards to formulate all the protection they can. A **conscientious work ethic** undergirds their still more conscientious efforts at protecting others. They will work long hours and seem never to tire at tasks for which they are given little praise or encouragement. What others would avoid they do with the conscientiousness of a saint.

Society is blessed by ISFJs who are the true **defenders** of the poor. But remember these guardians are not only the protectors of the poor, they work diligently for the rights of all people and, as parents, ISFJs are formidable champions for the rights of their children. They teach **doing the right thing** and endeavor to model it for all, including their children. But the right thing is not the apex of behavior; rather, doing the right thing for the right reason is much more honorable, and this they recognize.

With **consistency,** they meet their own obligations and model a life of responsible behavior perhaps more completely than the other SJs. **Personal sacrifice** is all in the cause of duty for them. The spirit that drives this **guardian angel** activity is a devotion that displays their conviction that people must control the outcome of a world that is given into their hands. They are **controllers**. With that controlling nature comes the tendency to sink into worry and operate by Murphy's law — if anything can go wrong it will — so they set those rules in place to offset whatever failure of the system they can.

ISFJs are **thorough,** and you can't get much past them. They share the sharp eyes of the ISTJ, and being all about their five senses, they become **skilled observers** of all that is happening in their world. Taking note of the details, they tend to be **accurate in their assessments,** and therefore can be trusted as reporters, social watchdogs, and executors of the routines and systems that guard our world. A **painstaking attitude** fuels this thorough accurate observation of others and makes them excellent quality control agents.

ISFJs exhibit **patience with details** and pursue those who bend the rules and infringe the rights of others. No one wants this dog on his scent. Their patient approach creates a **tenacity** that stabilizes a project. You can depend on their seeing the matter through to the end. They are **perceptive** and will, with what looks like an intuition but is more of a sharp, perceptive use of their senses, detect the beginnings of breakdown in a system or detect a wayward intent in people.

Perhaps you have noted an overriding **interest in people** in the ISFJ at the expense of a concern for the finer details of technology. To the ISFJ, things are of insignificant concern and need less of their attention. Technology also can take care of itself. Toward people, however, they are really **loyal** and are trusted as wardens. **People's feelings** and concerns touch them and gain their attention before the impersonal facts, and they are considerate with warmth that promises the loyal care of these benefactors. Social rank is honored with all the time-honored trappings celebrating the journey of life, such as birthdays, anniversaries, etc. Heirlooms and antiques often intrigue them and they care for them with patience. Like all SJs, they are homemakers.

New gadgets are not prized like the **old traditional methods** of the past, the ones that in their opinion don't fail. Constant **change is unnerving** and can cause an ISFJ to be disoriented at times. Frugality is a result of their responsible attitude. They operate their budgets with care and protect their dollars, saving for a rainy day. And this is done to protect, again, from any future disaster that might make all their efforts a failure. It is the desire to do all they can to assure the darker side of life is kept at bay.

These champions of others and of a protective way of living are often not valued and can be misunderstood, making them the footstool of society. They deserve more.

Some Areas for Growth

- Learn to change to new concepts and ideas.
- Openness. Keep your mind open, befriending people of different persuasions.
- Prevent being undervalued; assert your needs.
- Personal care. Look after your own interests and needs since you so liberally give to others
- Optimism. Factor more optimism into your life
- Strengths. Use your strengths wisely
- Self-esteem. Take pride in what you accomplish
- Overuse of strengths. Be aware of overusing your protective attitude
- Learn comfort with logic and its application.
- Avoid becoming overcommitted and slavish in supporting authorities and their policies.
- Refrain from complaining and negative attitudes.
- Look ahead with a well-thought-out plan.
- Avoid becoming immersed with the past and its memories at the neglect of the present and future
- Joy. Lighten up! Try being happy without being serious.

Stress for the ISFJ

ISFJs take on the stresses of those who seem to be unfairly treated. It becomes their stress, and if they succeed in helping the unfortunate, they feel rewarded, but if they run into opposition and red tape that hinders their drive to succeed, they begin to stress. Frustrated goals are a real danger for them.

Because right is right and wrong is wrong, when the shades of gray appear in the pursuit of their goals for themselves or others, they become militant and angry. Feelings can begin to dominate and direct their logic. They feel the mounting pressure that all SJs feel when they are not able to control their world and thunder clouds of panic can set in. Order is needed, and if order does not obey to the measure that they approve, stress mounts.

When they feel that they can't protect those they care about, they can easily succumb to the mood I mentioned that if anything can go wrong, it will. They can turn negative, and negativity alone is a stress to a human system that is made to function positively. Worry and undue anxiety can disrupt their ability to function in everyday matters. The stress of worry takes them down.

If their mind is set on some project, they can work without any end in sight and endlessly pursue an unrealistic goal. The lack of success as they doggedly pursue their goal will in itself build unbearable stress. Also, if they are patronized with no respect for their convictions they can easily become resentful and bitter. Stress for the ISFJ is mainly caused by their allowing the negative to become the focus and worry the method, with anxiety and hurt the result.

Therefore, they can, with a positive approach, develop a more hopeful and optimistic approach to life. They must learn to know where the limits are for their influence, time, and abilities and live within them. If they see life as more than protection of others and of ideals, but also as an opportunity to enjoy all things, they de-stress.

The suggestion to the ISFJ is to break from their duties for a moment for themselves and provide plenty of time to have fun with others. When life seems unfair, remember that it is. And each of us must learn to deal with unfairness. It is part of maturing and growing up.

The Child

This child can appear sensitive and troubled by his emotions. When others are hurt he will seek to protect, show sympathy, and remedy the situation with an obvious determination. A disturbed or nonfunctioning family can cause much pain for the ISFJ and result in much fighting to try to make things more equitable.

This child must be taught the positive and realistic ways to solve human issues and problems. The energy spent on and generated by worry needs to be directed to positive activities. The sense of fairness, which is idealistic in the ISFJ, makes him pursue endlessly the struggle for more equity among his friends. He can be hurt in the struggle by those who are not affected by unfair treatment and who look down on the ISFJ as though the is weak in some way.

Parenting this child through the maze of emotions he entertain about himself and others is not an easy task. However, keeping close to him and making sure you are sympathetic to his feelings while seeking to direct him positively and realistically is the path to success.

Teach him to be who he is but not to overuse this strengths. Overuse is a concern, and overprotection is a weakness that, if not handled in childhood, will be a persistent cause of stress and irritation as an adult. Therefore, always lead him to the positive and optimistic view of life and implant hope when he is upset about his world.

The Achilles Heel

Concern can be a force that takes us captive. When it does, it can turn us in the direction of negative behavior that eats away at our peace, happiness, and hope. Concerns can become obsessions. Hurting for others can do as much damage as hurting for ourselves. And all this is unsettling and makes the ISFJ's foundations quake. An overuse of concern is what we must guard against.

Worry, over-concern, and negativism are their Achilles heels, and the destroyers of the tender, loving, and extremely kind ISFJs. Faith in the ultimate triumph of good, optimism about life, and a firm hope that will not be overwhelmed by doubt and pessimism is the path for these protectors of society.

Summary

(This short summary can be a quick way of understanding the central themes of this type. Also, it can be used to check an assessment's accuracy by asking the person if they concur with a majority of these statements. Simply put, does it sound like them?)

ISFJs are loyal and supportive to the extreme. They are the world's great protectors of people's rights and welfare. When you have become an ISFJ's concern they will protect you from the dangers and the ill intentions of others. Keeping you safe and cared for brings them great satisfaction and they protect their family and friends with a saintly fervor.

Sometimes they appear and feel like lone rangers monitoring their world, but they crave a social acceptance. Shy and reserved, but not when they protect others, they can be under-appreciated, and this causes them pain because they listen so intently to people's needs and implement so faithfully. Their hearts are warm, their style frugal and down to earth, and their work habits are drenched in seriousness. ISFJs are unselfish, agreeable, but not always open to change, since it rocks their world and creates feelings of insecurity.

The NT Temperament

ENTP

ENTPs are **innovative** by nature, always searching for a better way of doing things. On first meeting, they seem to promise a stimulating encounter, and certainly an engaging one. There is something easygoing about them, even though they can become intimidating. **Laid back with their options open,** they can appear warm and welcoming.

Open-mindedness is an expected trait of the ENTP, and any closed-mindedness in life or in argument will stir in them a negative response, which is likely to be a sincere attempt to crush other's dogmatism with their logic. Their open-mindedness gives them a scanning ability as they listen and then, after they detect a flaw in an argument, it helps them search for their retort all at the same time.

Their minds are quick to discern faults in an argument. But this quick and alert mind can be too fast for its own good, and when it is, it loses its advantage over the more reflective thinker or the one who carefully checks off the details or processes the options. Speed of mind means for them **speed of response,** and like the mentally fast, tactical SP, they are exceedingly quick at finding the best strategy.

With opponents in the world of argument, they are very competitive, playing the game of one-upmanship with skill like no other. Because of their extroverted nature, they are **outspoken and opinionated**. They may well argue just for the fun of it and take whatever side of the argument seems attractive to them although they are not necessarily convinced of its truth themselves.

Like all the NTs, they are **strategic** in their thinking, all the time running ahead in their minds to solve the "what ifs" that any good strategy insists must be thought of and accounted for. ENTPs are several jumps ahead of where they appear to be. Life for them is a strategic battle with ever-changing odds. Because they are all about their minds, as Plato would have them, they are always devising **theories** to combat or circumnavigate the contingencies of life.

Strategy requires **ingenuity**, cleverness, originality and the mind of the NT is bored by what has already been discovered or used, passionately searching for the new and the innovative. Resourcefulness of mind can make them good at many things.

However, these **original thinkers** can be caught neglecting old or routine assignments. Anything that is new is a magnet and the old routine is boring, to say the least. It makes them feel limited by unnecessary demands, and their life of creative adventure into a world that offers endless possibilities is thwarted. They must press on in life. Problems need solving and they are drawn to solve them. Solving them is the ENTP's fun. In the challenge there is a thrill, and in the solution there is a reward, a deep feeling of fulfillment as though they have been affirmed in their mental adventure.

Most of their adventures are mental. They do not share the unbridled daring of the SP in the physical world. Courage? Yes, it is there, but it is a **mental courage** to always find what lies over the hill of difficulty that their mind is encountering, and to venture without any promise of success. As we said, strategizing and finding hidden options is the mental activity that makes them **invent, design, and conceive** new things.

From an early age, they are intrigued with building and making things. Toys that can be fashioned into their mental images, and gadgets that can do a task differently or expertly fascinates them. As they age, this adventurous mind never gives up its curious nature. They become invaluable in companies that want to find and market new ideas and gadgets, but they must be given their freedom to think in unexplored territories.

In the workplace they are **nonconformists**. Let them find their own path. Pilot projects with the freedom they provide will enthuse them. You need only say to the ENTP, "it can't be done," and you have secured their commitment.

In all of their ventures, they keep an eye on what is **pragmatic**. It must work or be of some practical use. Since so much of what we humans do is less than efficient, the ENTP takes on the challenge of making us ever more efficient with their inventions. They are the **efficiency** experts. It grieves them to have to do something in a redundant way and submit to the bane of incompetence. They resist any inefficient method with obvious disdain. They, like all NTs, are concerned with improving the means to the end.

When they seem always to be obsessed with the new and the different, they give you the feeling that they are on a mission. Those less willing to change criticize their obsession. ENTPs don't take criticism lying down. Their response is usually to argue the foolishness of their critic. They will find logical reasons why they are right and the other person wrong. In the pursuit of winning, sometimes their arguments will be less than logical, but as long as they confuse or defeat the critic they are acceptable for that occasion. As arguers, they are only surpassed by the INTP who finds argument an end in itself.

From youth, their **inquisitiveness** is a marked feature of their lives. "Why" is perhaps the most important word in the English language to them. "Why" leads to understanding and understanding, to new ways. And how they overuse it as kids, trying to penetrate the meanings of their world!

Technology interests them, but it is never an end in itself. It is merely a tool used to generate the means to produce the product. Keirsey reminds us that whereas the INTPs see their theory or design as an end in itself, the ENTPs see it as a means to an end. If they fail at providing a solution, they can eventually give up, unwilling to do the hard work of more careful preparation.

Curiosity may lead anywhere, so they do not usually make a detailed plan of their new invention. An ever-curious mind only needs a starting point, an idea that will develop with what they find on the way to the formation of the reality. Therefore, they are not the great theorists; rather, they are the thinkers that fly by the seat of their pants, guided by the need for a solution to their open-mindedness and their ever-expanding ideas along the way.

In case it sounds like they are all about things and not people, we need to note their expertise in understanding **human systems,** such as how the politics of an organization or the efficiency of a reporting system can be improved. They will hunt out the inefficiencies and map a better way for human interactions to evolve.

With friends, ENTPs display their easygoing attitude and are less critical and argumentative, except in fun. They can appear lighthearted with **lively humor**. Their conversations are invigorating, exploring all ideas that might be expressed. **Stimulating** is the word for their interactions with those near to them.

Some Areas for Growth

- Appropriate use of strengths. Live in the ingeniousness of your own strengths without their overuse.
- Develop sensitivity to the feelings and needs of others.
- Avoid becoming harsh, rude, or irritating to others
- Play the game of life fairly and with mutual respect.
- Refrain from being too pushy and without sensitivity, challenging others inappropriately.
- Overcome the appearance of being arrogant or combative in your dismissal of others and their ideas.
- Avoid an open-mindedness that lacks structure to keep it focused.
- An open mind will avoid obsession over your ideas to the exclusion of others.
- Mental pathways. Remember, logic is not the only path to truth.
- Commendation. Learn to praise the intelligences of others even when it isn't your own idea.
- Avoid moving from one interest to another with little purpose.
- Be less critical/Critical of others who you do not deem as smart as yourself.
- Learn to see the importance of emotions and people's feelings.
- Love. Develop love, caring, and compassion for others and tolerance for their differences.

Stress for the ENTP

For all NTs, stress is generated when in some way they fail or can't seem to make their mark. ENTPs, with their active minds, think up great ideas, but when they find it hard to do the follow-through necessary to implement them, they falter and the stress of seeing their ideas waste away can be considerable. Their minds are quick, and they play the game of oneupmanship well, but often as a foil to hide their lack of skills at making their ideas a praiseworthy reality.

The nature of self-image is to motivate and give us reason to proceed. A feeling of powerlessness in making the ENTP's ideas come to fruition can create self-doubt, which is never expressed but is nonetheless destructive to confidence. They need to partner with an SJ who will make things happen for them, but this will mean sharing the glory, and some are not willing to do that. Hence, they get stuck in a highly creative but unproductive backwater. When stressed and full of self-doubt, making the right decisions to create desirable success is the path to the healthy motivation they need.

Because ideas that don't see the light of success are often criticized, the ENTP can be the object of ridicule. Also, the well-meaning but hurtful remarks of a recognized authority in the field can be cause for the collapse of their self-confidence. Even though they will not confess to having emotions, they remain sensitive to the critique of others, especially those who they might respect. Emotions really do play a central role in their stress.

Furthermore, if the ENTP has been critical of others (which they are not shy in doing), their lack of ability to complete all the mundane steps that will bring their conceptions to completion can in turn make them easy targets for those they have criticized.

They may tend to move on too quickly to another of their frequent ideas in the hope that this one will succeed, but they never really stop to face the cause of their failure. Relationships are not left unscathed either. In an effort to bolster their faltering self-image, they can turn negative and blame their closest ally for the failure of their relationships, creating yet another stress factor in their lives.

The Child

Frustration caused by the same stress as we have just seen in the adult ENTP can inflict the child who has great ideas, but little patience with follow-through. The lack of approval from parents to the flurry of ideas that go nowhere can damage the child's self-image early in life. However, natural pride keeps him coming back with more ingenious ideas. When feeling the sting of a lack of importance among his friends because no one seems to think his ingeniousness has any real practical worth, he can take to becoming a revengeful, self-defeating critic of

The InnerKinetics of Type

others. In this, they can succeed easily because of their sharp observations of the weaknesses in other people's thinking.

This child is best parented with ready approval of his ingenious ideas and of his quick thinking, plus the help to learn how to follow through. That will require teaching patience, and lessons in delayed gratification will help. The child must also be taught to share the praise for a successful project when he teams with those who have the skills to make ideas flower into real life. Shared praise is better than no praise.

His disdain of having to admit failure will cause a wilting self-image to go underground undetected. Keep a sharp eye open to undesirable behavior toward others that will flag you, the parent, of a crushed self-image. You may also note his repeated attempts to take others down. It is strange that as humans we call ourselves intelligent creatures, yet we find our self-importance in reducing the value of others. Negative attacks in this case never produce positive results.

Managing a healthy self-esteem and avoiding the destruction of overconfidence and pride is the parent's main task as they raise this extremely masterful little thinker. Find the narrow path between healthy self-confidence and unhealthy pride.

The Achilles Heel

Self-doubt is the Achilles heel of the ENTP. Regardless of what we think about the importance of self-esteem, it operates regardless of whether we think it does and lowers the effectiveness of even the most brilliant and mentally sharp among us. No one can escape its clutches, and when in its vice grip, we cannot escape without rooting out our self-doubt and replacing it with healthy self-belief.

As we have seen, ENTPs can seek to escape by uncovering the logical failures of others, but this kind of relief is short lived and not without its damaging side effects. Relationships fail and acceptance among others is jettisoned by a critical sprit.

The ENTP's true place in society must be appreciated. It is not a superiority that sees them as above the importance of others. It is recognition of the true strengths of others and a healthy, balanced understanding of where they fit into the pattern of these strengths as equal, needed, and significant, but not greater than others or independent of them.

ENTPs can best help themselves by finding a confidant or coach that can help them live to the reality of their own strengths and not find comfort in looking down on others. Appreciation of another's abilities is the place to start. The more appreciation of others that the ENTP can express, the more they help themselves to be appreciated.

Summary

(This short summary can be a quick way of understanding the central themes of this type. Also, it can be used to check an assessment's accuracy by asking the person if they concur with a majority of these statements. Simply put, does it sound like them?)

ENTPs are logical, clever, original, and inventive. Their ingenuity enables them to think through an idea and build prototypes, always wanting to see their inventions launched. This creative genius is where they make their greatest contribution to the world, and it is what they enjoy most. Their curious mind and skeptical attitude combine to make them great analyzers of almost any theoretical system. They probe and search for pragmatic answers, spurred by an innovative spirit and a desire to keep their options open to all incoming data. This also creates a confidence that they will be able to find a solution to any problem that may arise. Simply let them point themselves in a direction and something will come out of their passionate process.

ENTPs, as you recall, like to argue and discuss, since they are all about their minds. With an eye for strategy in debates, they are seldom at a loss for which direction to go, and they easily a plan to win. If they feel trapped, patience is a strong point. They will persist in a seemingly relaxed game, sure that they will find their way to victory. If you are part of their world, this drive can become tiring.

Cool-tempered at times and usually calm, their easy-going approach to people is seen as engaging and in good humor. Relationships can display an on-off nature and emotions are not easily recognized.

ENTJ

As **instinctive leaders,** ENTJs build organizations around themselves, organizing people and programs always with a clear goal in mind. **Taking charge** is normal to them. They will, however, express their surprise at being in charge, not noticing that they are the ones who took over and lead in the first place. They do not move if they don't have a **well-defined goal.** They are quick to see possible weak spots in an organization and if they do, they will step in and take over the direction of the task rather than delegate to a person of unknown qualifications. It's the **end result** that matters. Gathering all the human resources available and focusing everyone on a mutual goal is where they excel. They are natural **mobilizers** of people and resources. Therefore, they can be chosen to conduct massive campaigns and initiate the mobilization of forces, such as in the case of war.

Their astuteness in knowing what to do when faced with contingencies is led by a **demanding logic** and an ability to conceptualize where the organization is going and where it should go. Their theories are developed into **firm plans** for action. Inefficient procedures, inadequate policies, and illogical steps are ruthlessly discarded and transformed into a smooth-running system. The ENTJ as a leader will tend to herd people in the direction they have planned for the organization and do so mostly with people's willingness since they trust the purposeful leadership style and the confidence of the ENTJ. An ENTJ will bring a surge of hope to a dying organization.

ENTJs, instead of making their own strategic plans, will often adopt the plans of others and show their skills in implementing them with their own practical strategic skills at **making things happen.** They keep the **vision** of the organization firmly in mind, both short and long range goals. With their extroverted thinking and nature they are the best of all the NTs at taking charge of people and implementing plans.

Business, military, education, and the complex field of politics attracts them. They bring leadership and impersonal skills to running and coordinating the resources of such organizations. Decisions are made on impersonal, objective data woven into a strategy for implementation. People must fit the plan rather the plan fitting the people. **Tough-minded** is a good word to describe their leadership style.

What, perhaps, they lack most is the ability to intuit the emotions of people and see emotional concerns as an important indicator of the need to alter their plans. This **impersonal, unemotional** side of leadership is what limits their otherwise clear advantages at being the best of all leaders. Therefore, they work best in an authoritative organization where they can take the lead and not worry about how some of their moves may create uneasy feelings in others.

They also use their thinking skills, applying them primarily to the external world, **decisively** forming actions and plans of how things should be done. These then become their own plans in the real world that they clearly communicate and then enforce on themselves and others with little leeway for error. Sometimes they may fail to consider all the options to a plan because their decisiveness has jumped the gun, and they act prematurely. It is hard for them to reverse such immature decisions.

Efficiency, competence, and logic must be honored and must be honored by all. Emotional responses are usually not facts that are concerning enough to change a plan. They run into trouble when they don't discern the importance of emotional flags. They are **frank, logical, analytical**, and can be critical in their assessments of another's motives and actions. **Assertiveness** can be their stock-in-trade means of dealing with such aberrations to the plan.

When an organization has problems they are keen solvers of its problems, provided emotional opposition to their plans is not an issue. They are **action-oriented** in all they do with the ability to persuade people of the virtues of their plans and, therefore, they often succeed in making things happen according to plan.

Public speaking is a natural, as is good reasoning abilities. They are well-informed and do not want to speak without knowing that they know what they are saying. The **pragmatic** nature of their minds keeps them relating well to people and their needs, and they lack nothing in clear oratorical skills. A love of learning and a desire to add to their knowledge is a lifelong pleasure. They are encouraged when asked to implement complicated systems because the more comprehensive and complicated the system, the greater the challenge to their innate skills.

When frustrated they can resort to **critical** attacks on subordinates or those who have some power over them.   Unfortunately, again, the emotional concerns of others are not noticed and not thought important enough to be addressed.   The solution is nearly always a better, more pragmatic plan. Also, they will resort to abrasive or cutting remarks toward their critics and give yet more commands with the expectation that the logic of the commands is alone enough to gain the submission of the opposition. In this they fail readily.

If an ENTJ is ideologically convinced, they will force their beliefs on others and not seem to notice the disconnect they are creating. It can be their leadership downfall with those who do not share their persuasions. They can also be **ingenious** in their pursuit of their goals but, as we have noted, ingenuity with a lack of intuition that deciphers the feelings of others can cause them to have difficulty. Unless their goals or belief systems say otherwise, they can be the best at reducing bureaucracy and lessoning the overhead of an organization.

Like the ENTP, they are **stimulating conversationalists,** energizing a casual relationship with **humor and confidence,** which they seldom lack. Conversations can take a turn for the worse when they resort to a skeptical attitude of the other person's ability or motives and, in true NT fashion, give the impression that they are better and more intelligent. They must watch the temptation to take firm control of the events and goals to the exclusion of the people's needs and opinions.

Some Areas for Growth

- Develop patience. Repeated mistakes are a nightmare to you and you.
- Sensitivity. Living in your strengths means not overusing them and being sensitive to the emotions of people.
- Emotions. Emotional intelligence is perhaps your greatest need.
- Insight. Be open to the subtle suggestions by others for change.
- Opinions of others. Consider that all people will not approve of your plans.
- Leadership.   Develop a concern to detect and react with positive changes when the followers are not following.

- Understanding. When dealing with others, discover their beliefs.
- Patience. Learn the skills of a less verbally aggressive approach to people's failures.
- Give attention to your personal life, especially the needs of family members
- Persona. People may want to see a more personal side to you; let them.
- Give others time. Avoid overusing your decisiveness and making decisions too speedily.
- Understand the need for introverts to process.
- Values. Since the means to the end is important to you, keep in touch with your values and moral compass.
- Learn to play. Time off is not time to work more.

Stress for the ENTJ

Stress is generated for the ENTJ when they can't figure out why people would, for some non-communicated reason, not follow the ENTJ's plan and/or try to thwart it. Even though the ENTJ can fashion or adopt the best of plans, constructed in all their needed detail, all it takes is one obstructive person to raise their stress level to the point of sleepless nights. Then all their work and effort teeters at the very point of success. This is somewhat ironical in a type that is so skilled and concerned with leading people.

Stress eats at the ENTJ at this point because they mostly lack the emotional intelligence and people skills to deal with what they perceive as unreasonable people or emotional resistance in those they lead. In taking a hard stance as the only way to solve the problem of stubborn resistance more stress, sometimes of a very disturbing nature, often results. ENTJs are "marshalers" of all resources. They form long-range plans that deal with all the understood contingencies, but the contingency of human resistance is for them the ultimate stressful challenge. To have a long-range plan destroyed by one key figure and not be able to handle it and save the plan, makes the ENTJ turn to other pastures in the hope of more favorable results.

The tendency to apply pressure can sometimes result in disdaining or ignoring the person who does not want to participate. This, however, can seal the fate of their plan and create unbearable stress. People view plans as less important than their own desires. Why people are doing what they are doing is the knowledge that will lead to the tact that finds favorable solutions for the ENTJ.

People's feelings have to be seen as just another contingency, and ways to direct and manage those feelings is what the ENTJ needs. Also, an understanding of when others see the ENTJ's leadership as controlling is what the ENTJ needs to develop to avoid stress.

To avert most stress, the ENTJ needs to acquire greater listening skills that not only hear but understand the emotions of others as well as how their leadership is perceived by others. To utilize all resources including people effectively (and the ENTJ is an efficiency expert), they must have control over all the factors: time, people, material resources, finances, schedules, policies, procedures, plus hiring and firing. If they don't have the authority or power to direct all these things, their complicated plan can fail, and then they slump into despair and guilt when they see how they have failed. To work under anyone else who is inefficient and scatterbrained will also induce unbearable stress.

Diversification of leading and teaching opportunities helps reduce stress because it changes focus. Continual learning will not only suggest better practices, but if the learning is focused on understanding people and developing emotional intelligence, the gain can be significant in bolstering confidence.

The Child

Perhaps you have noticed the strong drive of the little ENTJ. They lead because they must. Therefore, as they are trying to understand their world and the "strange" people in it, they often try to force others to do what they can see is the best thing to do. When force works, it reinforces the belief that this is the path they must tread. If they are too successful with force, they develop a habit of making people do what they want.

The playground can often reveal this developing habit, and when it is seen it must be redirected. Try teaching them better ways of getting people to follow them, like asking, respecting others, forming a team, and always considering how other people feel. Keep showing them that how people feel is a contingency in their plans that can make or break their success.

Being all about efficiency, the parent will also suffer their scrutiny and become the target of their demands. "Why don't you do it this way?" will be heard all too often. This is, again, an opportunity not to get mad and irritated at the child but to explain and make sure they understand how to handle people. The strength of spotting inefficiencies and finding better ways should not be suppressed but directed.

When the little ENTJ is stressed, depressed, and feeling guilty, a dual approach can produce good results. First, they need to feel a little of the guilt of having failed to help them understand that something in their behavior needs adjustment. But, second, they do not need to sink into depression over their failures with people. They need to be lovingly and kindly taught how to be more effective. This way we develop the strength and avert its misuse.

Likewise, the pride of the ENTJ is not to be removed; rather it is to be modified to show a strong and healthy self-confidence without an obnoxious " I'm better than you" attitude. Little ENTJs are going to run into resistance. It is healthy since it is a teacher. So use all cases of resistance as opportunities for positive parenting.

The Achilles Heel

Overconfidence can be the path to the Achilles heel of the ENTJ. Perhaps we can best express it as a detachment from the emotional understanding of others. When they get disconnected with others, they can then fall into a state of despair, which they usually exit by finding some other focus for their skills to give them a lift. This doesn't, however, result in learning how to manage their Achilles heel.

They must carefully watch disconnections from others since these are the needed flags they must read to stop and modify their plans. Overconfidence is a subtle Achilles heel. It's "under-the-radar" nature leads to it not being noticed readily and, even when things go wrong, it is still not seen as a possible cause of the ENTJ's depression and derailment.

Summary

(This short summary can be a quick way of understanding the central themes of this type. Also, it can be used to check an assessment's accuracy by asking the person if they concur with a majority of these statements. Simply put, does it sound like them?)

ENTJs are renowned for being very effective at maximizing the resources at their command and heading the cause they lead in a positive well-thought-out direction. As natural leaders of people, everything must be planned and the plan communicated effectively to the people because people can be independent operators, ruining the effectiveness of the plan. This commanding and coordinated leadership is something they do outstandingly. They breathe confidence, and others gain strength in their bold leadership. Also, building strength by forging new partnerships is usually a means to the end.

One project is seldom enough, however. They can manage complexity and multitask well. They do not fear conflict but will sometimes overlook the emotions and beliefs of others, placing themselves in jeopardy.

Strategy, order, efficiency (they, too, are efficiency experts), and consistency makes them supreme pragmatists. If they are in charge they will take the reigns willingly and, without hesitation, forge ahead single-mindedly. All steps in their winning strategy are logically sequential and designed for effectiveness. Their extroverted nature makes them engaging with a noticeable warmth if things are going well. This can make them very attractive leaders.

INTP

Of all the NTs, these are the ones who can become most **obsessed with their ideas**. They tend to play with ideas, ever open to new data and ever refining them. Therefore, they live in their heads, as do all NTs and NFs.

When we understand this **intense, logical internalization** of their lives, it is no surprise that they appear **quiet and reserved**. When they let down their guard with close friends, they can tend to open up too dramatically as though it is the release of pent up desire to be more socially connected. They can be very connected, but only with those who share their passions or their ideas.

They have an **architectural** bent and live for the satisfaction of designing. **Designing** is putting things in ingenious order to create something of beauty. It can be designing masterpieces, such as wonderful buildings, bridges, plazas, or theoretical systems of any sort. Designing is also shuffling ideas, and all this is done in the activity of their minds.

They have, perhaps, powers of **concentration** as great as any type and more than some, and they engage in the practice of it daily. Because of this they are often loaners, working in **private** at their drafting tables or computers. When they emerge, it is after they have reached a stage where concentration can take a break.

Their love of **theoretical systems** involves them in the typical NT strengths, such as analysis, logic, skepticism, and pragmatism. They are as **pragmatic** as the other NT types. They tenaciously hold onto the practical ideas of which they take ownership once they have created them. To wedge an INTP from their designs is difficult indeed. They can show an unwillingness to change details in their creation that, in their minds, are essential to the mental beauty of the piece, even when asked to do so by the one who is paying for their work. Along with this love of theoretical systems and theories is a love of **scientific interests**.

All problems must be solved by careful **analysis** of the problem and its causes and then by the rigid use of **logic**. These are the ones who are fascinated with logic and its application to argument. They will argue about anything, if for no other reason than the fun of argument and the practice it gives them. Even when their premises are not well-founded, they will argue nonetheless.

Skilled at argument, they focus on winning, and anything less is not enough. When losing in an argument, they will turn the subject matter so that they can win.

Social problems soon mount up and they may withdraw from social activity into their world of ideas. Small-talk bores them. Frivolous parties in which they are not able to exercise their rational skills don't excite them either. Perhaps another issue hinders their social engagement: They tend to have well-defined or narrow interests, and finding others who can engage them in discussion about these interests does not readily happen. They also can become so obsessed with their ideas and complicated theoretical creations that others feel as though they have nothing to contribute and are left out. But for the INTP, they must wrestle with their complicated ideas until they fully understand them.

Unlike the other NTs, they are not impressed with external reality. The external world is more distant to their minds. Theories and ideas crowd the mental real estate.

As with all NTs, **emotion is not valued** and if emotion is displayed, it will be met with a quiet disdain or a cryptic comment. They can become unfamiliar with their own emotions and when their emotions do erupt, they find it very difficult to manage them as they escalate into an inner tantrum of sorts.

When they don't understand, they simply close off and turn to another theme rather than get angry and frustrated. They can't design or construct something abstract or non-abstract if they don't understand. Other **options are open** to them and all they need is to find them.

What can label them and hurt them most is an **arrogance** and an intellectual snobbery that distorts their own opinion of themselves and others. However, it is an interesting twist that they can listen to the man on the street and adopt his ideas if they find them useful, while rejecting the greatest authority's ideas without concern.

Demotivation can be a problem since if they become loaners, and if their long labor and ingenious design is rejected and found unworthy of people's interest, they can fall into a state that destroys all of their drive and desire. It is sad to see this in an NT and it is not common. They return from the depths of despair to believe again in their mission of removing **inconsistencies.** They ingeniously create a functioning artifice of beauty, whether a physical structure or a theoretical marvel.

Some Areas for Growth

- Develop an appreciation for the place emotion takes in life and its rewarding characteristics.
- Sensitivity. Become more sensitive to the needs and feelings of others.
- People skills. Improve your people skills to maximize relationship possibilities.
- Motivation. Increase motivation and find a practical use for your talents.
- Learn that just because it is not logical, it is not wrong; rigid thinking can exclude a multitude of facts.
- Remember that questions are open-ended and gather data, whereas criticism is closed and shuts down the flow of data.
- Discover your own interests and develop them.
- Mundane matters. Knuckle down to the realities of life, such as bill-paying and taking care of health.
- Negativity. Take care not to be excessively critical and negative of others.
- Feedback. Keep your ideas practical and useful; get feedback from others to aid your evaluation.
- Availability. Withdrawing and keeping to yourself can be counterproductive.
- Social skills. Remember that life is social and psychological as well as a logical exercise.
- Lightheartedness. Enjoy life as fun, not just as competition.
- Senses. It's okay to enjoy sensory experiences, so go walk in the rain.
- Develop your intuition. An overemphasis on logic can cause you to neglect the development of your intuition.

• Appropriateness. Limit and learn when to appropriately engage in verbal arguments.

Stress for the INTP

Once again, as with the ENTP, their mental capabilities can be frustrated by the inability to follow through and make things happen in the real world. It is more of a problem for the INTP than the ENTP. They are commonly frustrated by the lack of passion and ability to enact the details. However, some do not realize that this is the cause of stress. Stress of significant magnitude can and does result. They can plunge into anger and direct it at whoever is near, since they cannot bear the anger being directed at themselves. It leaves them with the self-judgment that they are not smart enough to make things happen. Not being smart enough is, for many INTPs, an impossibility. Yet they can't make their cherished ideas happen, at times, without help.

INTPs are caught on the horns of a dilemma. They are independent and don't want to ask for help. Yet to be successful, they need help. Unfortunately for many, they let the matter sit with no solution rather than ask for help, and then their stress builds inwardly, forcing them to inappropriate behavior in extreme cases. Truthfully, they often do not understand why it is that they choose not to call for help. Their lives sit unmotivated and motionless when this happens.

When in personal relationships they are criticized or doubted or lose respect, they truly fall into a state of stress, feel powerless to change it, and adopt a negative approach to their critics. If not praised and constantly encouraged, relationships can become a drag. Although the INTP has great intellectual powers, they lack the skill to handle people for the benefit of all concerned unless they have learned good techniques. When they do act in the interests of others and show that they need others, they become superb creative partners.

INTPs are not logistical giants. They can even fail at Logistics 101. They need the dedicated help of people who are logistical and who can arrange the implementation of their ideas. An unwillingness to let others order and dissect their plans can be the beginning of their stress factors.

They must learn to enjoy life and others, which can help them interact and feel better about including others in their lives. But the real issue is in taking a hard look inside and dealing with the pride of being self sufficient. Self-sufficiency is a worthy strength, but it is also not an absolute need since we are humans, dependent to some degree on each other. Learning how to communicate when stressed and opening up to express their need is something they can do to lower stress and find solutions that will eventually eliminate stress.

The Child

Relationships and how to handle and value them is the major training ground the parent should consider for their little INTP. If the young INTP can learn to value relationships, not just for what they get out of them but for the way they can make a positive difference in the lives of others, they are well-equipped to form healthy unions.

The skills to make and maintain healthy relationships need to be taught as well. Skills such as showing others that they are important, equal, valuable contributors to the INTP's life, are basic lessons. The little INTP, though convinced of his superiority over others in mental issues, must not show it. The way to avoid showing it is to learn to appreciate others as equals. "I must think of myself as equal to all I meet but not better than they are" is a starting place.

Consideration of others ranks high for subject matter. So do appreciation and non-condescending love. Giving of ourselves in love leads the way to social competence.

The Achilles Heel

For the INTPs, the Achilles heel is overcoming the independence that keeps them from including others in their lives as equals in intelligence and ability. The INTP is not a complete package. Like all of us, they need others. They must realize that the overuse of independence and intellectual pride can keep them from utilizing the help of others.

Dependence and equality is sometimes a hard thing for people to swallow. No distraction or activity will solve this problem. Self-knowledge and understanding that leads to an "aha" moment, followed by an appreciation of their strengths and a realization of where, when, and how they are overused, is the path to wholeness and success.

Summary

(This short summary can be a quick way of understanding the central themes of this type. Also, it can be used to check an assessment's accuracy by asking the person if they concur with a majority of these statements. Simply put, does it sound like them?)

INTPs are the architects of ideas and physical structures. When useful, both have amazing potential to improve the life of humans. INTPs design masterpieces, but they seldom take the same time and ingenuity to design their lives. They can become obsessed with analysis and detail. Their imagination, developed within the bounds of reason, keeps them forever searching for new patterns and ideas.

The way people think and should think fascinates them and makes them engage in debate with a fervor that no other type can match. They approach their opponent with the confidence of a veteran, even if they are a neophyte. Their debating skills are legendary. Intelligence is treasured and worshipped, sometimes producing arrogance.

With an unmatched curiosity they approach the world seeking to analyze it, figure it out, and then explain its intricacies to all. And their easygoing reference to time shuts out the annoying interference of deadlines.

Analysis and design are productive partners and they use both with skill. Autonomy and an intense individualism can make them seem preoccupied and distant.

Forgetting appointments can be an issue with their clientele and mates. Sometimes shy, and in debate mostly aggressive, however, they remain removed from the mainstream of society.

INTJ

Presenting a calm, **confident**, assured, and **decisive** face to the world, INTJs seem to be holding it all together, and they are — with mental determination. They are **good thinkers** and often show an inclination to be **original** thinkers too.

Their minds work strategically, fashioning a plan with forethought for both the things they have to achieve and the **contingencies** that may occur and how they might affect their plan. When contingencies do occur, they inevitably have a plan B and operate it. Plan B will also have the goal firmly in mind and trace a path back to the original plan if at all possible.

Long-range plans are complex and comprised of many steps, and INTJs revel in the task of keeping each step in a **logical order**. Of all the types, these are the best minds at **analysis** and **strategy**. If any event occurs that they did not foresee, the impact on their pride and self-image can be considerable. "How could they, with their mental acuity, have missed it?" they wonder. It is their high standards of **competence** and performance to which they hold themselves that, if not achieved, brings them down, but not without a quick recovery.

They are observed by others as being proud and **arrogant** at times. It's this characteristic that powers their quick recovery. The pride arises from the obvious success they have at what they do. A feeling of **intellectual superiority** can also be seen in all NTs. From the earliest days the child has often been reported as having said to the parent, "I'm more intelligent than you." INTJs are all about their minds, and the feeling that they are better thinkers than others can push its way to the surface and become obvious.

They are **pragmatic** in all they do. Their theories must have some real application and work in real life. They deal with things and people sensibly and **realistically** and always with practical purposes in mind. Even though they are lost in their minds most of the time, they make all theories relate practically to the real world outside of their minds and, therefore, keep their feet solidly on the ground. Fantasy has no appeal to them, and even their imagination is kept within the boundaries of pragmatism and realism.

Skepticism is a basic tool that these planners use constantly. Nothing must be accepted until proven to them to be true or essential to their goals. Doubting everything is a way to evaluate things and analyze their value. **Curiosity** and success drive this skepticism in the INTJs, and it is seen in them at its most intense application. Their drive won't rest until they have seen the **successful application** of their ideas. Add to this a **determination** that stirs all their motivational forces and they can become very narrow-minded. But it is this **intense focus** that is the reason for their success and, therefore, they do not regard a determined skepticism as having negative qualities like some of the other types do.

To understand the INTJ, we must factor in an **independence** that makes them likely loners in their research and study. Any dependence on others saps some of their motivation. Also, everything **must make sense** to them. If it makes sense to others and not to them, it still does not make sense. "Sense," to the INTJs, is logic and reason together with what fits their standards for the project and is affirmed by their interpretation of the facts. The authority behind the facts is of little concern to them as long as they are convinced that the facts are real.

INTJs prefer to make **long-range plans**. It is the long-range aspect that creates the need for complex strategy. In this search for a long-term strategy, they show great skill in finding the patterns to all events and thoughts. In the patterns they find the logic to carve the best path to their goals. **Efficiency**, no waste of resources, and pragmatic purposes are their principles that guide them.

INTJs are driven by their plans and ideas. Once they have fashioned their strategy, it becomes their child to see to full fruition and success. The drive will keep them at the task for days or years until it is accomplished and released. **Social problems** plague them because others observe their interest in their ideas as excessive and exclusive of the care that relationships demand. Family and spouse can be left on the back burner for too long.

One thing poses them difficulty in all this planning: they see emotions and people's feelings as facts of life that are less demanding of honor and thoughtful treatment. **Emotional unintelligence,** for the INTJs (as for all NTs), is not a matter of having to control their emotions; this they do well. It is a matter of valuing emotions as equal factors in life and in their plans.

INTJs can be guilty of wondering why a human does not perform as they expect and criticizing the person for it, creating many a disconnection between their plan and the people who must perform it. The INTJ's plan is seen by others to be lacking in emotional intelligence. The obsessive, compelling drive to see their plan succeed can also strap blinders on their vision, excluding the feelings of others whose feelings might thwart it.

These strategists are **organizers** of their own thoughts and of their execution. They carefully sort out all the facts that they can muster, and they delight in the process. Then they apply **ingenuity** that is unequaled, and out of disorder appear sense and consistency. Hence, they can be **stringent leaders,** stepping forward to take the lead when they see others as incapable of making their plans live up to the standards theINTJ had in mind. They are, however, content to work in the background unless inefficiency rears its head.

There is a **self-confidence** about INTJs that is greater than in all the other NTs. It leads to a clear definition of their goals that reveals their firmly-held purpose. They are **opinionated,** largely because they have spent long hours doing their research and gaining confidence in their theories, and they are not shy in giving that impression to others.

Thoroughness in research and patience in analyzing all available data, along with detachment, clarity of thinking, conciseness of ideas, objectivity, insightfulness, and the ability to synthesize very divergent concepts are some of their greatest strengths.

They can make **devoted mates,** but first they must know that the person they want in their lives is worthy of them. They are also very proud of a successful and independent child.

Some Areas for Growth

- Develop a more sympathetic understanding of the intelligence of emotions.
- Consider and include personal data as relevant data.
- Control, but don't exclude mundane matters.
- Strength appreciation.   Maximize your strengths, but become appreciative of the strengths of others.
- Listen to your intuition so you do not exclude facts that on first glance were not relevant.
- Delegate.   Your project needs helpers, so recruit people who complement your strengths and believe in your ideas.
- Remain open to ideas outside of your ideological boundaries, also to those opposed to your convictions to avoid ill-made decisions.
- Obtain feedback to keep your thoughts relevant and realistic.
- Humility. Recognize and avoid an air of superiority that turns many off.
- Avoid intellectual quibbles that can consume your time and obscure your vision.
- Close-mindedness. Refrain from a stubborn insistence on your ideas that can be seen as an unbending attitude.
- Appreciation. Learn to give praise readily, even though to you it is only due when your high standards are met.
- Social intelligence. Develop a social life that is rewarding to others and to yourself.
- Share. Open your heart to someone who can be a trusted confidant.
- People skills. Develop people skills; people are humans like you.
- Experiences. Broaden your life's experiences; it will keep your mind fresh.
- Independence. Temper your fierce independence since we are all social creatures, dependent on others for many of our needs
- Relationships. Focus on relationship issues and warmly express your feelings

Stress for the INTJ

Those who are goal-oriented find their pressures coming from the process of achieving their goals. A theoretically-minded person is creating new ideas or things in a virtual world and trying to translate their concepts and plans into a practical world of actions and people.

This is an agenda for stress. Too many things are beyond control. Yet the theory is logical and complete in their mind, and the INTJ stresses over his inability to control all the options and make what he perceive as a logical, needed idea from seeing the light of day.

As with the ENTJ, the control of people is the biggest frustration. If some plan that benefits people and is thoroughly logical and reasonable is stymied by illogical considerations, the INTJ is left with only a few options. Sternly ram the project through (if they have the power and authority to do so), or try to convince the "illogical" objectors of their mental inadequacies, or withdraw from it all and seek another more fertile or welcoming opportunity.

However, one other option remains that the INTJ does not often pursue. Since the objections of people are mostly emotional concerns, why not address these concerns with an understanding of people's needs and show them your willingness to mold the plan to accommodate those needs if possible. The INTJ believes in their logic so intensely that this option feels to them like a "surrender" to other people's "illogical" thoughts. Why adjust the strategy just to pacify the emotions of others? In a world where feelings are unimportant, this is a reasonable complaint, but where feelings are all a part of the facts and contingencies that a plan must provide for, it is a reasonable requirement — a need.

The INTJ's stress comes not from a lack of understanding the emotions of other people as much as from a lack of appreciating them. Emotions are subjective issues, and it is hard to plan for subjective contingencies. The INTJs' upset and annoyance is easy to understand. The solutions to their stress lie in the way ' they handle their own feelings and judgments, too.

In forming a strategy, INTJs can become fiercely perfectionistic and insist on the gathering of every possible piece of data just to be complete in their survey. Adopting a "what's wrong with you" attitude to their team of workers when one or more fall below the INTJ's standards can quickly create an atmosphere of stress and less than a productive response.

Under all these pressures an INTJ can fall into self-doubt. That can lead anywhere, but always to the detriment of the project. Therefore, INTJs prefer to go it alone and not be bothered by the idiosyncrasies of people or of the doubtful supplies of resources managed by others.

The adjustments they can make can include the following:
- Lighten up the atmosphere and, while emphasizing that the project is all important, show that the people and their needs are more important.
- Include in their personal strategy for successful completion of the project touches of humor, and emphasize the need for the people to have fun together on the way to success.
- Develop effective listening so that the necessary feedback about how the people feel is constantly received.

The Child

The young INTJ is a world of new ideas. There is always a better way, in his view, of doing things, even to the way you hold a pen or write a sentence. Frustration with others who don't see the benefits he see in his new ideas can be quickly observed by the parent. Again, the path of positive parenting is to develop the strength without encouraging its overuse.

Direct the INTJ's drive to make all things new and, since he has this intense drive to guide his ideas into pragmatic realities as well, help him to do so with concern for others and patience with those who don't see it as clearly as he does.

The INTJ needs to learn that others are not dumber than he is but are concerned with other issues that may be affected by the INTJs new way of doing things. The battle of helping him see that his strategies must include the feelings of other people as legitimate facts — facts the plan must address — is the more advanced, but necessary, training a parent can give an INTJ child.

When frustrated because they don't have the right building blocks or enough "Lego" pieces, the INTJ can be challenged to do the impossible and make it happen without the desired pieces. Challenging him to do better and find the creativeness that is in him can be an effective control of the frustration.

Tell him you want him to be who he is and come up with a solution to the problem. If you don't, and you simply supply the right blocks or the needed Lego pieces, he will grow up to expect that when he faces a similar problem as an adult and is stymied, he will not be able to proceed without the needed pieces. His creativity will not have been developed as it could.

Don't forget, you can suggest that the solution to the problem the child faces may be to modify the goal or change some of the strategy to make available supplies adequate. Change the design, perhaps, or find ways for one piece to do the work of two. As a parent you will be stretched with parenting an INTJ, and that isn't all bad.

The Achilles Heel

The Achilles heel of the INTJs is self-doubt, which is a real killer of their potential greatness. All types *can* be great. This one *must* be great or fail. The bar is set high but, as with the INFJ, it is not constantly set higher when not reached.

Self-doubt can come from many directions, but in the case of the INTJ, it is coming from the frustration of not being able to control his environment and make what he conceives happen in the real world.
When failure is the cause of self-doubt, getting success in one form or another is the best solution to lift him out of periods of self-doubt. Pride is affected by failures and the INTJs sometimes have to see themselves as less successful in the present moment, accepting failures in order to be more successful later.

Summary

(This short summary can be a quick way of understanding the central themes of this type. Also, it can be used to check an assessment's accuracy by asking the person if they concur with a majority of these statements. Simply put, does it sound like them?)

INTJs are "conceptualizers" and the best contingency planners. They typically do not desire leadership, but if their plan is not being executed as they conceive it should be, they will jump in and lead. As planners, they plan long-term with superb strategy and logical consistency, having a plan A, B, C, etc., firmly in place to take care of unforeseen issues that may arise.

First, they must know their goal and devise a clear vision. They then think and plan within the framework of a system that has a theory they shape and fashion. Fiercely independent, they are skilled at finding the reasons behind things and at using those reasons in defense of their theories. To some, they can be intimidating with their confidence and convictions thrust out there as a challenge to all comers.

Their calm exterior, a thing they admire, is an attempt at self-mastery. Emotional disturbances are disruptive to them, and they avoid them in themselves like the plague. If they engage someone in discussion, they find it hard to know when to stop. A cool exterior and an air of superiority is also often valued.

ENTJs may have difficulty in relationships, but they love to be on the leading edge of research and mental adventure. They are noted for their tunnel vision, love of logic, and calculating, analytical minds.

The NF Temperament

ENFP

ENFPs are very **warm** and seek to connect with people, and that can mean anyone. They make a successful connection almost immediately, crossing into the other person's heart with ease. What makes their warmth so attractive is the **enthusiasm**, even an **effervescence**, that obviously drives them, and this is seen even when they are more reserved in their approach to people. They give the impression that they are truly **willing to help** and befriend almost anyone. Most are likely to be a little late to appointments, but this is soon forgotten in the warmth of the encounter.

ENFPs are therefore outgoing and **vivacious** and perhaps the most fascinated with people of all the temperaments. As a result, **talking** is a refined art. They seem to be the bridge to the SP temperament, exhibiting a **high spirit** and a love of fun and excitement. Since the NF is second only to the SP in **optimism,** this can be expected.

The driving emotions in the ENFP are **passion** and **enthusiasm**. **Excitement** and **optimism,** for which they are also remembered are cut from the same emotional cloth, and this seems only to increase their passion for life. It is an ENFP maxim that life must not be wasted. They must wring the last drop of excitement from the present moment, just like the SP does, except for the fact that the ENFP's excitement must have **meaning**. If the fun and frolicking has no meaning, it is soon abandoned for something that does, like serious conversation. This is why the ENFP can be the life of the party one moment, and the next moment she may be sitting in a corner, engrossed in a meaningful exchange with an introvert.

ENFPs feed off s**ocial encounters** and find a very real satisfaction in being a valued part of someone else's life. *Meaning,* to them, is being **significant to others** and sought after by them. They are tuned to their emotions, and powerful **emotional experiences** are the essence of life to them. Nothing must be missed. Everything must be felt to the full and passed on with fervor to others.

Emotions are deep and wide — encompassing all there is in life. Exploring these surges of emotion that shape them is where their adventure begins and ends. Life is a search for ever more **meaningful events**.

Their social life, if lacking, can lead immediately to the first phases of depression. They find it hard to help others in depression, seemingly because they find it difficult to be so near a spirit that dampens their own.

Life can be a puzzle for them if they find it hard to connect with others or if others reject or neglect them. **Life is people.** They have **quick minds** that are exceptional at finding a solution to a people problem in particular. In this way they resemble the quick mind of the NT, but the mental interest is of a totally different nature — people and emotions. Because these two focus points make up most of the important interactions of life for the ENFP, their minds are well-practiced in diplomatic skills.

Myers-Briggs calls them *ingenious.* However, since the word is more commonly used of clever inventions than it is of solving people's problems, I would prefer to call them **imaginative, resourceful,** and **perceptive**, with great sensitivity toward people.

In their intuition they are eidetic, creating unusually vivid mental images of people's emotional states. This **intuition** is well-advanced in the ENFPs and can lead them to be in easy touch with influences from the immaterial world of both good and bad. Like anything else, intuition, if focused on too exclusively, can lead to wrong insights that are known to mislead the ENFP at times. However, more so than most NFs, they can, with their intuitive skills, detect what is in another person and know the emotions that are driving them. These are the things on which they will base their conversations and their attempts to help. Because some people think that their unspoken feelings are not able to be seen by others, the ENFP's intuitive knowledge of their private thoughts can be unnerving, to say the least.

Empathy is also strong in ENFPs. Entering into the hearts of the hurt and unfairly treated and sharing their pain is commonplace. They are truly loving and caring hearts.

The P in their profile points to their living in the moment and their ability to **improvise** and show **extreme adaptability,** meeting whatever is the **spontaneous** need of the moment. If surprised by someone's reaction they can turn in an instant and adjust to what they sense is the need.

This leads to their not being ready preparer, and they will avoid preparing in advance for a conversation, preferring to rely on their native skills of improvisation. When they find themselves doing something that is not advised, they can quickly find compelling reasons to support their actions. Their skills and natural strengths enable them to do almost anything that interests them in the world of people.

ENFPs are not flighty. They are full of deep **convictions** that drive their lives and that you are likely to learn about even in a short conversation. There is a fervor about their beliefs and a guilt that follows when their actions are inconsistent with their beliefs. One of their certainties is that truth should always be mixed with love, and they sincerely believe we must **speak the truth in love**.

I mentioned that they are talkative, and in support of this tendency they have developed a skilled use of **language**. The nuances of speech and the choice of the simple and fitting word make them masters of inspiring and moving language. They can excel in public speaking, using the art of **persuasion** with a depth of meaning that reaches all people.

You can't tell an ENFPs how to dress or what they should be or do to impress. They are **individualistic** to the core. They must reveal the image they have for themselves, not what is expected or advised. There is a personal vision within them of what their integrity should look like, and this is the **authentic** person they would have you remember.

Usually, ENFPs are very keen, **probing observers** of others. But adding to the astute use of their five senses, they rely mainly on their intuitive insights. It is a probing use of both their physical eyes and the eyes of their minds.

Emotions play a large role in the ENFP's life. All their relationships are infused with their passion. No emotion is small to the ENFP since they feel compelled to respond to whatever they read about their world.

Hurt is a major concern since they are hurt so much of the time, and that ruins their present moment and all it has to offer. With no way to deflect the hurts of others, they defend themselves by either withdrawing or delivering a verbal broadside that can frighten the most callous opponent away. However, with all the problems emotions cause them, the ENFPs are a bundle of rewarding, rich feelings that warm them and attract us all.

Stephen Montgomery, in his book, *People Patterns*, comments that they are **positive, passionate people,** and that is perhaps the best summary of their nature and type. The focus of life, for the ENFPs, is people. Goodness, since they are **ethically oriented**, is also important, and they have this bold expectation that things will go right. Things usually do, and this makes them believe that they can indeed control their lives with their optimistic and intuitive drives.

Some Areas for Growth

- Decisiveness. Develop a decisiveness that keeps you from repeatedly returning to the entanglement of your feelings.
- Analysis. Develop your logical skills of analysis.
- Values. Find a helpful balance between rational and value-based decisions.
- Evaluating others. Give people a second evaluation.
- Optimism. Keep your optimism in the face of disappointing circumstances.
- Hope. Keep yourself inspired to avoid a serious letdown — good things are coming.
- Focus. Learn to focus when events distract you and scatter your feelings.
- Reactions. Avoid rebellious reactions when frustrated and hurt.
- Environment. Your work environment needs to encourage engaging with people with creative freedom.
- Preparations. Seek to prepare a little more for things while still depending on your impulsive insights.
- Details. Find help in taking care of details.
- Overextended. Overextension of your resources must be avoided or depression will set in quickly.
- Limitations. Learn to say "no."

- Patience. Try to understand other people's intentions and use patience with those who irritate you.
- Strengths. Appreciate and live in your strengths.
- Integrity. Be who you are designed to be; don't limit yourself.
- Self esteem. Keep that self-image high.
- Knowledge. Get to know people and their temperaments.

Stress for the ENFP

Being disconnected is a major stress. ENFPs are all about meaningful, soulful connections and are severely stressed when this is not a reality in their lives. All NFs are stressed to a great degree when stressed at all.

Being all about people, ENFPs and all NFs stress over disharmony or the simple lack of relationships in which to find harmony. ENFPs are fed by the actions and encounters of the moment. Without sufficient confirmation of successful relationships, they wilt easily and fall into self-doubt and self-rebuke. They stress over what they might or must have done wrong, or not done, to cause their feelings of loneliness and depression.

They also stress over hopelessness, helplessness, the feeling of emptiness, and all such inner emotions. If the future is not full of possibilities, they can stress.

When stressed, the ENFPs lose much sleep and toss wildly at night, restless and directionless. A sense of disorientation makes them lose motivation. Causes (such as the mission of the company they work for or the objectives of their church or philanthropic organization) that are not faithfully followed and that lose their purpose are draining, and they feel the loss of integrity as a personal loss.

The ideal for the ENFPs is connections with harmony and meaning, making the loss of the ideal feel like the loss of their world. Such intense entanglements with their world makes the ENFPs vulnerable. Friends that let them down or fail to meet expectations cause major collapses. The present moment must have its fill of significance, causing them to sparkle and light up with obvious pleasure. If it doesn't, a depression (which for others is out of proportion to the letdown) sets in and can last for days.

ENFPs are stressed when people don't see the need for personal growth and development. They can't imagine a person not being exercised over their own betterment as do all NFs. Their high energy is another cause of stress, not only because of the demands such high activity imposes but also because, when it seems to have no opportunity for outlet, they fall into anxiety about themselves and all they have done or might have done or not done. A fierce self-evaluation plagues them. I would be remiss in not mentioning that loss of any sort can plunge the ENFP into a sudden state of stress out of which it is hard to extract them. They must extract themselves by coming to terms with their emotions.

Whenever the expectations that they have of others are not met, they take it personally, even down to the details of some project that is not enthusiastically embraced. To keep stress within acceptable limits, they must not try to be less idealistic or introspective. The focus needs to be on an idealism and introspection that is positive as much or more than it is negative. Stress for the ENFPs is not dismissed by a lowering of their standards either, for that they cannot endure without becoming someone other than who they are. Stress is to be managed and what is harmful and hurtful needs to be detected and, with the help of rationality, eliminated.

Every dark cloud has its silver lining. In this conviction and with the application of faith is their ability to manage mounting stress. Physical exercise is calming and restoring. The reestablishing of hope and future possibilities cannot be over-stressed as a major source of decompression.

The Child

The ENFP child's bubbling hyperactivity and desire for people should be obvious to the parent. But he needs approval, regardless of his extroverted nature. Approval for who he is matters much more to him than approval for what he achieves. Constant affirmation of his being loved and special are tonics for emotional health that the ENFP can't live without. If he doesn't get it, he will usually ask to see if it is forthcoming. The mood of the little ENFP will change instantly when he senses connection or disconnection in this relationships.

ENFPs are very sensitive and can be helped or hurt by the least change in fortune or relationship. As a parent, you may wonder if you will ever be able to meet their every emotional change. You don't have to. Just rest assured that if positive affirmations are plentiful, you will succeed. They must struggle a little to find out how to mange their emotions, so when you do not respond with help, it is not the end of the world.

Prevention means keeping their lives full of significance and meaningful reactions with people, animals, nature, learning, books, and dreams. Treat them gently and keep the emotional temperature of the home warm and without angry outbursts. They don't help anyhow. The parent needs to employ lots of calm explanation and instruction.

Perhaps more than any other temperament, the NFs need the model of a home of peace and harmony, but not without positive excitement and adventure. Creating this model may be strenuous, but it will pay off in a bonding of child to parent.

The Achilles Heel

Disconnections in relationships trouble the ENFPs the most. Such disconnections can be with others as well as with themselves. If depressed, they may tell you of their inner loss of touch with reality and their sense of being disconnected from their world and themselves, wondering all the time if they are "all right." They feel somewhat removed from the world when they have no meaningful relationships, as though they are walking through a world in which they don't belong. Since they live for every meaningful experience in the moment, this is like being cut off from what is needed most in life.

Restoring the connections or finding new ones is the best healing salve. But the ability to deal with the emotional impact of disconnectedness must be learned. This is achieved by developing intelligent emotions that don't lose sight of their personal worth when they suffer a loss and by not by entertaining the hurtful emotions so willingly. Replaying the loss is not at all helpful and will take them into the sad land of depression faster than anything else. If new relationships or reconnections with the existing ones are not possible, a feeling of closeness with family or a confidant is usually enough to recreate the flow of positive emotions.

Summary

(This short summary can be a quick way of understanding the central themes of this type. Also, it can be used to check an assessment's accuracy by asking the person if they concur with a majority of these statements. Simply put, does it sound like them?)

ENFPs are high-spirited, full of enthusiasm, the most vivacious of all the types, and they certainly charm us all. They are all about people and need interactions with people to keep them charged. But to the ENFP, people are experienced in the present moment. It is in the present context that they connect and drain the last drop of meaningful encounter from their experiences.

They approach people and things optimistically and, as a result, will light up your life. Their intuitive antennas are constantly activated, receiving all transmissions, and they then create their perceptions of them. They listen to what is not being said, and with uncanny accuracy, they intuitively interpret these unspoken meanings.

Idealistic, empathetic, and living their fantasies through the realities of life, they are always hoping for the magical moment of soul-mating. They need to succeed and win or life is boring, so they champion causes and lead with a powerful influence. Spontaneity feeds their creativity. Personal values and a longing for integrity drive their decisions.

ENFPs display a restlessness in finding the real fulfillment for their lives, and they can't imagine it without people. They are self-expressionists, authentic, probing, and emotionally intense.

ENFJ

Wherever they go, ENFJs **teach**. Friends, family, and contacts are all taught the principles of a good relationship and a successful life. And they do it with flare, love, and **obvious warmth**. Their **powers of influence** are considerable. As teachers of groups and individual, they set their minds on helping you to your potential, sparing nothing of their effort to accomplish this goal. They have a brilliance in being able to formulate an answer, on the spur of the moment, to a question or situation that is erudite, appropriate, and drives the point home. **Analogy** is one of their stock-in-trade ways of illuminating a truth, as it is also for the other NFs.

As children they can be seen teaching and directing their mates and always influencing them. They lead the activities and herd their playmates together, always instructing. **People skills** are woven into their every attempt to teach, and these skills alone make them stand out as **natural educators**. When leading group discussions, a smooth tact and a natural ease underlines their basic design as leaders.

As you might expect, their skill with **language** is noteworthy, not their vocabulary or their knowledge of other languages necessarily, but their inborn skill with the use of just the right word and its right intonation at the right moment. This enhances their teaching ability. Words such as articulate, dramatic, expressive, and touching are descriptive of their talk.

ENFJs are **magnetic** people. The sense you have of immediately being connected to them makes them hard to resist because of what their trusting extroverted attitude exudes and their **optimistic expectation** that you will do what they want or suggest, not for the minute thinking you would do otherwise. If you resist their welcome, the surprise on their face is enough to make you reconsider. ENFJs are instantly **responsive** to you, focusing on you with a warm intensity that excludes for the moment all other people, things, and interests. That loving force-field you feel entraps you. They usually have a large to very large circle of friends, all of whom are made to feel that they are the ENFJ's best friend. The magnetism pulls you in and you don't notice your own reciprocal warmth that they have drawn out of you.

They want to be empowered and **influence positively** every encounter they make. With their children, workmates, and friends they want to feel in control of themselves and confident in the use of all their influential strengths. When they master themselves and find the thrill of purpose and a fulfilling direction for their lives, ENFJs forge confidently ahead in life, content.

Just as the ENFP has **many friends** and is exuberantly warm, the ENFJ, with no less warmth but maybe a little less vivaciousness, gathers a cluster of friends by including each in her extended family. Both ENFPs and ENFJs are naturally **popular**. ENFJs may not be the life of the party, but they share their homes and their lives unstintingly and make you feel **unconditional acceptance**. People are also their world.

Sociable to a fault at times, they draw people who have suspicious purposes right into their circles. Experience, however, teaches them slowly that they should not trust all. When they are taken in, they react with a determined fury and shun that person like the plague. It is as though they say, "You spurn my love and I will punish you forever with my rejection."

Like all the NFs, their **emotions** are very responsive and strong, and when angered, they can flare with a frightening speed that makes anyone want to withdraw to a safe distance. People are emotional creatures, and the ENFJs are super-emotional. They can get hurt very easily and when they do, they find it difficult not to show their upset. Their faces darken and their feelings are easily read. All NFs have this problem, and the ENFJ is no exception. Their emotions are rich but also can be damaging in their relationships. Control is necessary.

In their social circles, and all the world is their circle, they are very **responsive** to people. Hence, they are intimately concerned with how others are feeling and what they are thinking. Anything that concerns you concerns them. It is evident that how they treat you has to do with how they perceive you feel and what your emotional state suggests you need.

Of all the types, none is more **empathetic** and caring than the ENFJ. Sympathy does not describe them; it is always a far more engaged empathy. Why your problem should not be theirs too does not even occur to them. Why they should not help you solve your problem and keep in contact until it is solved would not cross their minds. However, this outgoing empathy can be taxing, and they can easily be overwhelmed with the problems and concerns of others, leaving them at times feeling ill and totally drained. They must watch this.

A need stands out. These warm responsive types are in need of just as much love and care in return. Persistently **neglect returning their love** and they can leave you for another and not look back. **Harmony** in their relationships (which means an active two-way street, busy with obvious love) is an imperative in their intimate relationships. **Praise** is readily accepted, even though they will tell you they do not deserve it. Criticism had best be tactfully delivered and if not, they are as negatively responsive to it as they are positive to praise.

They are also **creative,** but mainly in their innate ability to solve complex problems and insightfully discuss complex issues. In conversation they can be very **stimulating,** and they always have a clear goal in their conversational intentions. You could never accuse them of not being sincere in their attempts to help you.

Their **idealism** upsets them at times, since they evaluate everyone as well as everything by an ideal standard and, of course, no one is perfect. This fall from grace can be very disconcerting to them. While the rosy glow of their expectations is pleasant for them and others notice it on their face, the letdown that they also show on their faces when expectations are dashed tells of the pain. Their faces are barometers, shining or clouding readily. Confidence is not as much a problem for the ENFJ as it is for the other NFs, but it is still not as vibrant as it is in the NTs.

ENFJs are **affectionate**, romantic, and in their relationships, always intuitive — sensing the feelings and thoughts of another, constantly seeking the knowledge of what is going on in the other person's mind and heart. They long for a **soul mate** and dream of perfection in their relationships. Disharmony is deadly.

Some Areas for Growth

- Trust. Trusting others can be overdone; use caution.
- Empathy.   Extreme empathetic involvement with other people's concerns must be limited to available energy and time or you may become sick
- Intuition. Your intuitive insights are helpful. Exercise them; don't let them scare you.
- Personal needs. In pleasing others, remember your own needs.
- Activity. Pace yourself. Extroverted activities can drain you because of your intense nature.
- Logic.   Develop a more logical analysis in the decision-making process.
- Personal values.   Remember to consider other values beside the personal ones in your decision-making.
- Honor feelings and intuitions; they must not be squelched.
- Hurt. If hurt, carefully analyze your hurt.
- Transparency. Your feelings are transparent, so understand that you are easily read at times.
- Relaxation. Because of your incessant drive, learn to relax
- Reactiveness. Work to become less reactive to criticism, whether real or only imagined
- Idealism.   Temper your over-exercised idealism; it may need understanding and management. You may find it hard to admit that your ideal person is less than ideal.
- False guilt. Avoid feeling guilty when you fail to help others
- Self-blame. Refrain from blaming yourself for disharmony in your relationships; analyze carefully and fairly
- Strengths. Live in the wisdom of your strengths
- Dreams are refreshing, but sometimes they conflict with the rewards of reality. Enjoy both.
- Knowledge. Get to know people and their temperaments.
- Influence. Study how to use your great influence.

Stress for the ENFJ

Feedback is the key element that stabilizes or stresses their world. Without meaningful approval and recognition of their labors to create harmony, happiness, and peace among family and friends, the ENFJ is plunged into gloom and self-doubt. What has happened to nullify their powers at building friendships and maintaining them, they wonder. And then they beat at their confidence while hope also flees.

The ENFJs show a tenacity to persist as strong as any type, but when they receive negative feedback, even no feedback, and when friends fade into the mists of their own self interests, the ENFJs feel a failure at life. Life is friends, family, and community. How can you give up on life easily? They can't, and life becomes an empty hole when they are not successful with friendships. Disagreements among their loved ones is also hard to bear. They take this personally too.

Stress also results from a lack of direction in life. They are advisors, teachers, and leaders in the world of friendships they have built. Without direction, they begin to lose touch with their world, and that means they turn on themselves, blaming the lack of fulfillment on their lack of ability. The problem of their career becoming drudgery and having to plow through the day in a bored state is a hazardous stress. Where is the evasive secret to feeling fulfilled, they ask themselves. Stress mounts for any unfulfilled ENFJ, as for all NFs, and the desperate search for satisfaction becomes fervent.

They exude a high level of activity and sense of urgency when they feel inspired. In such cases their influence is a force to be reckoned with and their purpose in life feels mature. They can burn out. Any obstacles that are placed in the path of their success during periods of inspirational power are resisted, but not without a feeling of disbelief. A surge of self-doubt and personal hurt accompanies all their efforts to break through these obstacles, which they see as the deliberate attempt to ruin something good. Anger and its stress ensues.

Over-empathizing with the hurts and needs of others can cause great stress because the ENFJs find it very hard to disengage and breathe for their own mental and emotional health. This stress can lead to their lives being spent for one concern, while other concerns and needs wait. The solutions to an ENFJ's stress are to refocus on all those who make up the inner circle of life and be all they can to them. The refocusing changes the mental landscape to a forecast of sunny days and pleasant weather again.

The Child

The child can be bossy. Trying to make everyone happy is a task too great to assume. We are responsible for our own happiness, not that of others. Teach the child to know the difference between doing all he can to make others happy and the feeling he must make others happy and be their friends.

You will find the little ENFJ trying to be the teacher of dolls, toy soldiers, and other children. If you are not watching, also of you, which is not all that bad because you can direct his goals and activities to learn where the appropriate limits are. If family relationships break down, you will have in this child your own in-house counselor. He is turned outward toward all others because of his extroversion, and this means the control of others feels like a need to him.

Love should be displayed often in these children, and they need as much, if not more, returned from the parents. Where they are loved, ENFJs are at home. Provide the opportunity for them to entertain their friends and keep friendships warm. Encourage all of their attempts to show love.

Because they can be so loving when they are not angered, you may not see the need for expressing your love. But remember, all displays of love toward you are also tests to see whether they are good enough to evoke your love in return.

The Achilles Heel

Taking the lack of approval as a clear message of their own failure in relationships can and will destroy the ENFJs quickly. They will seek other relationships or environments or attempt incessantly to gain the approval they are losing.

When they feel consummate rejection, they will turn away from that individual and not return. The hurt is too great to endure. Their intense focus on whoever they are engaged with in the present helps them forget the disappointments and disasters of the past, and this they welcome.

The path to avoidance of the Achilles heel is to proactively seek approval when it is not there in order to determine whether they need to change some behavior. Asking can be difficult for them, but to learn to ask if they are accepted and pleasing to others and then to believe the sincere response sets up a healthy device to ward off self-condemnation and the unnecessary loss of friendships. Their inwardness is both a blessing and a curse. Knowing when it is a curse saves the ENFJs much heartache.

Summary

(This short summary can be a quick way of understanding the central themes of this type. Also, it can be used to check an assessment's accuracy by asking the person if they concur with a majority of these statements. Simply put, does it sound like them?)

ENFJs succeed in the real world of relationships. They readily share their lives and, of course, their time. Making friends is a breeze. Friendly, warm, and always out there, ENFJs want to bond with you and grow together. Their intuition, like all NFs, is strong and focused more on the insights they regularly have of people. They are natural and very effective encouragers. Like the INFJs, they long to lead people to the realization of their dreams.

Teaching, especially groups, is a natural tendency in them. They are skilled at thinking creatively on their feet to answer, complete with metaphor and analogy, some puzzling question. They take their communications for granted and expect you have heard and approved just as they try to do for you.

As group leaders they excel because they have a knack for drawing each person out and using that person's potential. They are stimulating company, enthusiastic, empathetic, articulate, and they cast a spell over you. But don't create disharmony or you will be severed from their tender friendship until you adequately repent.

Soul-bonding is their dream. They need to be loved and will love with passion in return. If married to a non-loving partner, they hurt daily, and their whole persona changes with an evident suppression of their strengths.

INFP

Quiet and **reserved,** while showing a very pleasant face to the world, the INFP is an introverted NF with a unique recasting of the meaning of introversion. Introverted NFs have this **social,** outgoing, almost bubbly encounter when meeting people. They appear to be extroverts on first impressions. It's a cross between being reserved and being expressive. If the INFP and INFJ are saddened or depressed, they can appear very withdrawn when meeting them, and then you will be wondering if they are sad or reserved. Typically, they look like extroverts until they have been drained by too much social interaction. Then they wilt or withdraw to recharge.

A **curiosity** about all things, but especially about people, fuels the INFPs' observations, and they want to know what is going on inside other people's skins. They constantly search their own **intuitive** antennas to detect either good or harm and whether the person is safe material for a deeper relationship. In their quietness, INFPs are **observers** with a purpose. They wish to gather all the information they can (both intuitively and through their physical senses) about the person they are meeting to know if they should open up. INFPs can be very **closed**.

Self protection and nervousness about their **volatile emotions** is the reason. They must be given time to become comfortable with people. Their **warmth** and introversion suggest this need. They appear, as all NFs do, full of **trust** and love but with a shell that remains difficult to truly penetrate.

Emotions are a major concern to the INFPs. They get hurt easily as much by what people don't say as what they do say. We often refer to supersensitive people as having *thin skins,* but it is more a case of having no way of defending themselves against the hurts. When hurt, they withdraw physically or within themselves. When they explode, they hate themselves for it. Really, the INFP is a loving, tender, and remarkably warm individual who is a treasure to know.

INFPs are especially **loyal**. Once they have committed themselves, they feel bonded, and to break that tie seems sacrilegious to them. They will stay in a relationship through much emotional abuse without ever seriously considering an exit. One reason for this is their **idealism**. No NF is more idealistic than the INFP. Idealism carries with it not only the promise of a perfect relationship but also, after the hope has been dashed, the promise that it will rise again. With renewed hope, their idealism renews the contract and tries again. If they intuitively made a commitment, why would it be wrong? The struggle is deep and exhausting to have to walk away from an idealistic, intuitive choice.

The idealism extends to much more than relationships. Everything is idealistically envisioned. Even their own inner life lives under the eternal wish of the ideal. "Why are they so troubled?" they ask themselves. It wasn't supposed to be this way, was it? They long for the **inner peace** and calm that their idealistic view of how they should feel instructed them it would be in the first place. So their outer lives must always be congruent with their inner values and their inner lives congruent with their realities if they are to achieve this goal of peace. Their idealism seems limitless and is sacrificial.

Fantasy is a relief from the harshness and boredom of the world as Lewis Carroll (Charles Lutwidge Dodgson) so aptly displayed in *Alice in Wonderland*. INFPs live a life of realized fantasy, rescuing a world lost in its own serious realities and wounds.

A strong **ethical standard** guides their lives as well. They are very **accepting** of others and of new conditions if their values are not threatened. These can be their ethical and moral values as well as their personally chosen values for their own lives, both internal and external. If threatened, they will respond by withdrawing, or if the conflict is severe enough, with a frightening verbal attack.

The **purity** of their inner lives is of extreme importance to them. Often they will lay awake at night, searching for answers to the inner turmoil they are experiencing. Is it them? It nearly always is in part, they conclude, wary of fanning the fires that burn inside. Some live in

constant fear of the darkness that can seize them and carry them into the dungeons of its terrors.

To understand people and find ways to help them find their way through trouble and stress to finally discover their potential in life is an innate drive in the INFPs. The way they see they can lead people to this lofty goal is to bring **healing** and **wholeness** to them first. Inner healing leads to inner calm and peace. This is their vision for their lives and they feel extraordinarily fulfilled when they can help just one hurting soul. In this self-acclaimed occupation, they display a patience due perhaps to their laid back attitude and their belief that the right time will coincide with their plans. How can a person ever reach his potential while his mind is anything but peaceful, they wonder. Healing means the calming of the inner storms of guilt, doubt, self-doubt, and hurt. They dedicate themselves to helping those close to them to this inner bliss.

Wholeness is a holistic experience of life. It's a philosophical view of life. Life is made up of many parts, and if any of those parts are not synchronous with all the other parts, turmoil and trouble brew. **Internal harmony** is the INFP's lifelong quest and necessity. When it is not present and accounted for, depression and self-doubt quickly descend on them.

INFPs are quick to **discern possibilities,** although they are not always quick to grab them. They must process their feelings about each opportunity and then move when they feel comfortable. There is a delay and a desire to keep options open, even in the face of an urgent call to grasp an opportunity. Hence, they can often miss golden opportunities and they try to jump aboard when the train is leaving. This discerning of possibilities is again a result of their intuitive powers.

They come upon their mental discoveries more often by intuitive sensing that is strengthened by an active imagination than by logic or simple observation. Because of this, they can be invaluable at sighting new applications and new methods in dealing with people. They serve as **catalysts** in revealing the world of new ideas, not only about people but occasionally with all things. They are keenly **alert to people's feelings,** and this is one reason they can see the new person hidden in the emotions where most others don't even think to look.

A deep **empathy** surges in the mind and heart of the INFPs. They are the natural, in-depth emotional givers to those close to them and to any that may wander into their lives. Not even other NFs can care and empathize as much as the INFPs can. Think of Joan of Arc and any of the great lovers of those who need help.

It can be a **calling to mission,** ordaining them to the cause of love and practical help for all. They also can reach out with unusual love and awareness to the needs of some cause or group of people. This empathy often extends to all animals, and they can choose a life of training and caring for animals, some becoming scientists in search of understanding animals. Both a native intuition and empathy combine to make this a natural interest and a calling.

INFPs are **adaptable** and flexible, impulsive and spontaneous, making them all the more valuable at reaching into the world of personal **innovation**. It is a natural gift that also feeds their artistic abilities. They approach ideas with the NF's **global mind** and leave the details to others who are more earthbound in their thinking.

They show little concern for the things that give status and power to others, such as possessions and the trappings of wealth. The world is not a materialistic paradise but a place where right and wrong, health and hurt are confronted, and right and health matter supremely.

INFPs even feel **alienated** from their real world and think of themselves as just passing through. Childhood can be a sad time for NFs, and particularly for introverted NFs whose fantasies stand out as too "otherworldly" for parents. For some it is beaten out of them early in life, or so the parents hope. It never really leaves but remains to further disturb and make them feel they are somehow twisted and belong elsewhere. Why this world?

Can you be too happy, too content, and too peaceful? Perhaps, says the INFP, so they wait for the dark days to come (which they are convinced they deserve). Too much goodness can bring the clouds of evil — an interesting twist on "we reap what we sow."

Nurturing spouse and children alike, they hope for the best and often sink when a black cloud of doubt and **despair** forms. The INFP is a treasure, and it is sad that they all too often think that they are the cause of pain when they struggle so intently for the good.

Some Areas for Growth

- Depression.   Watch carefully for the onset of depression and discouragement, and take steps to avoid it.
- Understanding. Try to appreciate other people's beliefs that seem so strange to you.
- Reality. Keep in touch with reality and the world that is your external world.
- Relax. Keep health and physical exercise in your life because exercise is relaxing.
- Inwardness. Avoid becoming too inward; it can stunt your ability to help others.
- Motivation. Do what it takes to stay motivated.
- Making decisions. Decisions should be made with the combination of reason and emotion.
- Focus. You may need to be more centered and focused so as not to float about with your emotion.s
- Self protection. Develop other means of self-protection other than withdrawing.
- Avoid self-judgment; it can be a serious problem.
- Models. Find a hero or heroine and seek to emulate them.
- Planning. Learn to plan a little more.
- Delegation. Delegate to others your concerns about other people so they can help to share the load.
- Stress. When stressed, keep self-doubt at bay.
- Positive influences.   Focus on the positive and endeavor to be optimistic; avoid the dark side of life.

Stress for the INFP

When all their focused efforts at bringing healing and harmony to their environment are ignored or rejected, INFPs fall into critical and demanding ways, which is simply not typical of them. The quiet ones can feel as though they are not heard and, therefore, they feel the need of anger and loud denunciations to get through.   Great stress is the result in their relationships, and guilt mounts within them when they resort to anger. Failure is usually assured. The peace they long for has then become a world of upset and hurt. The road to peace and wholeness becomes much more difficult.

INFPs endure a lot before they explode or implode. The stress is at a high level for a long time before they show their upset or sometimes before they attempt to help or heal the broken relationships. Sometimes the stress develops at the early stage of their own perception of a damaged relationship when, in fact, they are the only ones as yet who suspect damage. A sensitive imagination that penetrates reality can produce a good deal of stress.

The manner in which they seek wholeness in their world can be the way to ensure the opposite. Wholeness is a state of peace and health, and therefore, is entirely positive. Nothing but positive methods and attitudes can achieve it.

Anger at being ignored is therefore a temptation and a trap for the INFPs into which they can fall too quickly. When they feel hurt, it is hard to feel loving and to proceed with peaceful methods such as loving your enemies. They must see that the hard road is the road to success. The road of negative responses is a certain road to disunity and war.

Being an idealist, the INFP is baited by their idealism into disappointment and discouragement. If they realize that to be an idealist is to aim at the ideal, expect the ideal, and be content with reality in a woefully inadequate world, they stress less.

To aim at the ideal results in a greater chance of coming near to the bull's-eye, so idealism is great. Self-understanding and patience with others who destroy our ideals does not come easily when our passion is so intense, but it is a must for health and success.

The Child

The little INFP is a quiet, loving child, and if his world is peaceful, he develops emotionally mature. Therefore, a quiet, peaceful home life can do wonders for him. Yelling and loud denunciations only activate his need to make the home peaceful himself and when he can't, he can become as angry and loud as the ones he wants to quiet.

The intuition of this child is very active, as is the INFJ, and if the parent is saying "I love you" when inwardly disturbed at the child, the child will not believe it. The child intuits the parent's inner condition and this is what molds the INFP child's behavior. The parent cannot hide successfully under any false front with an NF, especially an introverted NF.

To meet the needs of parenting, this child will require the remodeling of the parent. The parent does not have to be what she is not, but she does have to provide a calm, patient, loving model for the child.

Keep the volume down and that will cover a multitude of sins. The child will need training in emotional intelligence and in developing intelligent emotions.

The Achilles Heel

The ability to handle the stress of being ignored and put down for noble, worthy standards and values is ultimate success for the INFP. However, to be tripped up by these attitudes in others is their Achilles heel. Being ignored or made to feel worthless is an attack that the INFP finds great difficulty in dismissing.

The challenge of patience in wanting and producing the good in a world where the bad is glorified and modeled so often can wear the INFP down and make him lose all control.

A strong spiritual faith and a love that does not give up is the path to the INFPs being the healers of society and the salt of the earth. Hope must be nurtured and they do well to find someone who can be the constant support of all they admire and love.

Summary

(This short summary can be a quick way of understanding the central themes of this type. Also, it can be used to check an assessment's accuracy by asking the person if they concur with a majority of these statements. Simply put, does it sound like them?)

INFPs can seem to truly go with the flow, but the real beat of the drummer they march to is undetected deep inside. Pleasant, charming, and seemingly calm on the outside, they throb with intense empathy to the hurts and conflicts of others. They dream for and strive to resolve these conflicts and divisions among people. They get up each morning bent on creating wholeness and harmony, especially among their loved ones.

INFPs nurse a strong demand for personal integrity. Their thoughts and feelings must be in harmony with their values and beliefs. Otherwise they feel they are not operating holistically.

This struggle for perfection with themselves and their world creates a disturbing inner turmoil that is driven by their high demands and an active sense of guilt that lies close to the surface. INFPs are the wonderful self-appointed healers of their world.

Their intuition is often remarkable, knowing what lies behind what others are saying and doing. Mystery attracts them and they love to solve mysteries about people. Fiercely idealistic, truly selfless, humble and conscience-stricken for the slightest infringement, these adaptable and romantic lovers are highly attractive.

INFJ

As **mentors, speakers** and **coaches,** INFJs shine, always encouraging and teaching people to discover their potential and their personal worth. They are driven by this desire, which can become their dream.

As parents, they want to be mentors and encouragers more than disciplinarians. It is their ultimate dream to be **significant** in the lives of others, and with their driven nature, that means many others. Being "all things to all people" and "speaking the truth in love" are two maxims they readily adopt since people are their focus.

Both **leading others to maximize their lives** and to live in harmony with themselves and others give them ultimate satisfaction. **Personal growth** and development, the self-actualization of Maslow's hierarchy of needs, is truly their goal. They must become all that they can be and lead others to do the same.

As introverts, they share the same unique traits as the INFP. Their introversion can be very deep and the love of solitude is a longing that does not want to let go. In solitude, they nurture the skill of becoming significant thinkers.

The introversion brings with it the surprise of a **socially outgoing persona** that leads you to label them extroverts (see the first paragraph of the INFP). They are, together with the INFP, the engaging introverts. But they can wilt with too much people-contact and race to the solitude of their own sequestered nook. If anything, they are **driven**. It's the "J" that gives them a **determined**, responsible streak that makes some people mistake them for SJs.

This introversion also shapes the INFJ as the most **serious** of the NFs, displaying a studiousness and thoughtfulness that is driven by a natural bent for logic and what makes sense. This can cause you to think of them as NTs, so INFJs are confusing to identify. You will also see the search for joy and an element of optimistic hope in them when they are not depressed.

They can become **lifelong students,** always wanting to learn about whatever their current interest happens to be. The classic arts, psychology, religion, and all that has to do with understanding people anchors their studies and their influence in life.

Also, like NTs, they are all about their minds. INFJs can excel at cerebral matters, but not all do. Training and opportunity can make a big difference. Language fascinates most, but it is more the ability to carefully express themselves in an **influential and persuasive** manner. The emotive quality of words attracts them. Once they have overcome their reserve and nervousness (for some INFJs this is a high hurdle), they can make influential public speakers because of their emotional content combined with a studious mind. Meaningful one-on-one interactions stimulate them too. However, don't make them engage in meaningless chatter or small talk. They cannot abide it and will do what they can to escape.

INFJs and INTJs are often found in higher learning positions or places of influence where they crave all the time they can get **to study and improve their knowledge**. Keirsey has them as counselors, but in counseling, coaching or lecturing they are supremely **teachers** and advisors.

Confidence only comes to them when they know they know. Otherwise a **low self-image** prevails. Convictions run deep and they will express themselves with determination when they are convinced of their point of view.

They often garner respect for their **firm principles and ideas**. It can even rile them to have to listen to someone who has not done their homework and whose argument makes little sense or flaunts the rules of logic and sense. Why a person would talk before they think is hard for them to understand, although they do it occasionally themselves.

The surge of their **emotions** troubles them because of the strength of their feelings and their seemingly eternal struggle to manage them. They are constantly experiencing hurt. Their emotions range from a sincere love to a bitter rejection of the one who hurts them. INFJs are **supersensitive** to people and issues relating to people in particular. Anger is often felt and perhaps 95 percent of the time is due to hurt. They, like all NFs, have no shield against getting hurt and both anger and hurt flare together. Hence, they struggle to manage both at the same time and often don't do a good job of it in their own opinion, which leads them to **apologize profusely**. That usually causes another bout of **self-doubt,** which is all too common.

Perfectionist tendencies and a constant unfavorable comparing of themselves to others can lead to times of depression. Their low self-image also leads to depression, as you might imagine. Therefore, many INFJs never rise to the heights of their potential giftedness.

When they do succeed, it is in partly due to **perseverance**. When they set their minds on a task, it must be achieved to their own pitifully high standards or they are likely to remark, "Well, it wasn't much anyhow, and I didn't do very well at all." All NFs, when they have failed to satisfy their own standards, will set the bar higher next time, demanding more of themselves.

The INFJ is perhaps the worst at this **self insistence on perfection** unless they have owned defeat, and then they simply give up trying and resign themselves to mediocrity — sad. As ridiculous as this procedure may seem to be, it keeps them strongly motivated, always asking for more of themselves and can be the reason for any extraordinary achievements.

INFJs are **original thinkers,** tapping into their **imagination** and **intuition** to guide them to an understanding of people and life that will motivate the most unmotivated. Because of this and the insistence of their introversion to think through an issue before they say anything, they love to spend time **writing and shaping their thoughts** as perfectly as they can to influence others. Most are poetic in their expressions, relying on metaphor and analogy to make facts and their relationships more easily understood. Those who have not had the opportunity to learn writing skills still show a marked skill at expressing their emotions and thoughts on paper.

INFJs always put their best efforts into their work for the peace of knowing they did not shirk their responsibility and because they desperately want to please others. Their work ethic can best be described as **conscientious**. They will do whatever is called for at some sacrifice and if they do not please someone, they will then try to please another who crosses their path.

Failing to please their spouse or close friends can lead to self-flagellation and to seeing themselves as real failures. This all leads to a hatred of disharmony and conflict. They will do almost anything to create harmony with others.

Empathy, as in the INFP, is seen in the INFJ, although perhaps not quite as demanding of them. Empathy breeds concern for others and if they think that one of those close to them is being mistreated or is hurt, they will rise to forcibly do what it takes to defend them or help them. INFJs long for **soul-mates** and seek to bond with children and adults alike. Their warmth, which accompanies their empathy, creates a deeply **loving nature.** However, this plus the desire to please, can place blinders on their intuition.

INFJs are **passionate** to an extreme, but much of their passion is held inside and not shown for want of being misunderstood. It shows more as a **quiet forcefulness** that is fueled by a strong determination, and this makes them attempt to move mountains. If their passion is repudiated, they withdraw to try more fertile opportunities.

Although in many cases they do not seek leadership roles, they are likely to be sought out as leaders because of their passionate and clear **visions**, original ideas, and **determined leadership**. They always lead with a clear agenda and a vision for how best to serve the common good or the goals of the organization. Intuition plays a large part in their visions and their insights. They lead always, concerned as much for the people as the organization's goals and they are ever mindful of harmony or disharmony around them. An INFJ leader will be conscious of fairness and justice among the staff and will work for a true respect for all. If a worker is low on the status ladder, they will seek that person out to support and encourage them.

Not surprisingly they can experience premonitions and a vast array of what can be described as **psychic** phenomena. It is also not uncommon for an INFJ to realize that he knows the intentions and feelings of another person he has been focusing on before the person knows them himself. While being **intense listeners,** they often pick up insights and intuitions.

Here are some other pertinent facts about them. Hard to get to know, they can surprise you after decades in a relationship. They keep their thoughts and feelings to themselves unless provoked or hurt. They display vivid imaginations. They live very complicated lives and feel they are convoluted, not knowing all about themselves. This is true of all NFs. Their values are personally chosen and influence many of their decisions, yet they hope to be people of integrity. Argument and conflict are irritating and debate is not pleasant either. Romantic settings and relationships are felt to be essential to life. They are satisfied with the big questions of life being a mystery because they sense what questions must be beyond their understanding.

Some Areas for Growth

- Relaxation. Because of your incessant drive, learn to relax.
- Perfectionist tendencies. See your driven, perfectionist demands as a point to aim at rather than a standard that, if not reached, is failure.
- Emotional control. Carve a path between emotional excess and emotional suppression; it's called emotional management.
- Development of your strengths. Exercise your strengths to maximize your potential.
- Valuing your emotions. Always keep in touch with your emotions and their intelligent decisions.
- Vision. Develop your foresight and visionary abilities.
- Joy time. Learn to enjoy life; make happy choices.
- Intuition. Hone your interpretive and intuitive skills since they play a large part in your creativity.
- Responses. Withdrawal is not always the best response; learn other responses.
- Romance. Enjoy the many facets of romance; it is often simply bathing in the atmosphere of the moment.
- Personal space. Create a space all your own as your treasured retreat from stress.
- Communication. Communicate your reasoning or you will seem random and impulsive.
- Study. Keep learning; you are a lifetime student.
- Self doubt. Believe in yourself and your strengths; self-judgment and a low self-image can be a serious problem.
- Philosophy. Develop the philosopher in you.
- Language. Learn another language or master your own.
- Education. Develop your logical side; learn *how* to think — it's more important than *what* to think.

- Stress control. Recognize when the pressure is too great and take action to reduce it
- Depression. Watch carefully for the onset of depression and discouragement; use your strengths to rise above it.

Stress for the INFJ

The INFJs are subject to intense stress whenever they feel useless or that their life has no meaning and significance in this world. A low self-image plagues them and is an element in much of their stress. Their intuitive and reasoning abilities can be great, although not all use their strengths enough to maximize them. This is the NF that is both emotional and passionate while exhibiting a drive to have everything make sense and be reasonable and logical like the NT. Emotion and logic blend in the INFJs. Therefore, when their ideas are regarded as silly or off-base, the emotional dismissal and hurt is felt strongly. They are driven to be right, and for their visions and ideas to be repudiated or not listened to questions the core of who they feel they must be.

Stress results to the extent that they find they cannot work with those who do not at least acknowledge their intuitive abilities because the connections are hurtful. They also depend on their ability to persuade and when it fails them, they again feel something is wrong with them and that they are no good at the core and must admit it. Stress has then beaten them down, not the least their own denunciation of their worth. But the way out of this stress is the drive that will not seem to quit, and the next time their creative imagination and intuition comes up with another original idea, they are back championing it and making it work.

When up, they are up; when down, they are very down. Stress that is created by their strong drives is no stranger to them. Rather, they are the aliens in their world. Anger and depression, love and hope surge alternately in them. To find a position where they can execute their visions and ideas and their sense of justice and logic can help greatly.

Of all the NFs, they tend to punish themselves more, probably because of the strong drive to succeed and their horror of failure in relationships and in life. Disharmony in their own relationships is another powerful inducer of stress and anxiety.

Writing is a stress-reliever and the use of day dreaming to activate their imagination and change focus can do wonders. Connecting with nature in any way possible can turn things around too. Whatever they do, returning to their creativity reduces stress immediately.

The Child

The little INFJ is probably the most difficult to parent due to the volatility of extreme emotional pressures and hypersensitivity. This child can be extremely loving one moment and hateful the next as his emotions surge one way, then the other. However, for his mistakes and cruelty he will be very apologetic. Management of emotions can be, for some, a lesson that takes years to learn. But they must learn, and the parent should teach them early if possible.

Because INFJ children have such passion and are driven by their perfectionist and idealistic tendencies, they can chase one interest after another with abandon. To help them find their fulfilling direction can be challenging. It is best to develop their strengths and then they will detect for themselves what their purpose and satisfaction is.

Putting down their intuitive or imaginative strengths is damaging to both child and parent. They must be who they are. Withdrawal when their strengths are suppressed is the usual path, so watch for periods of withdrawal and question them to get to the root of their distress. A great deal of commendation and love is required,,and because of their low self-image, positive reinforcement of their worth is essential.

The Achilles Heel

The Achilles heel of the INFJs is self-degradation leading to self-doubt, self-flagellation, and depression. When a victim of this tendency, they cannot reach their potential, which only causes more of the same.

We can only lift our self-images ourselves. Blaming "causes" for low self-esteem is no help in the long run. The real answer is finding and living in the fulfillment of our strengths, and this should be the prime method to bring INFJs to self-actualization.

Summary

(This short summary can be a quick way of understanding the central themes of this type. Also, it can be used to check an assessment's accuracy by asking the person if they concur with a majority of these statements. Simply put, does it sound like them?)

INFJs live for personal growth, meaning, and significance. These things find their highest expression in this type and give them a strong feeling of who they are. They desire to please, but what is more important, they seek to develop others to the best they can be.

For the INFJs, life is a painting and we are the artists with colors and brushes, fashioning our dreams and destinies. INFJs excel at foresight and intuitive interpretations, creating visions and using their vivid imagination to sculpt the future.

Complicated themselves, they are expert diplomats, loving to solve the unsolvable differences between people. Therefore, they are natural mentors, teachers, and coaches, and when they overcome their reserve, they can be powerful speakers and influential leaders.

They live with a strong sense of direction. INFJs, like all NFs, are idealists and perfectionists, which can not only lead to great achievements but can give them unbearable stress. They are deep, logical thinkers, philosophic and metaphoric in their expressions, and sometimes excel at expressing themselves in the written word. INFJs are pleasant and social yet intensely private, keeping their inner life hidden. They are somewhat mysterious, being supersensitive and displaying vast intuitive powers. Also, they are poetic, creative, and lovers of harmony, seeking a mating of souls with those they love.

Conclusion

Everyone hears only what he understands.
~ Johann Wolfgang von Goethe

You are on a worthwhile, life-changing path. Investing in your life and in the lives of others will increase your happiness and effectiveness as well as theirs. We were made to find our way through the maze we call life. Mind, brain, and the drive to know naturally make us want to find out who we are and how we are made to live. Nothing is more rewarding than self-discovery except, perhaps, aiding another to the same insights.

Self-understanding is not a one-time event. We don't discover ourselves in one moment. We have what we can call "aha" moments, which are big strides in perceiving ourselves, but the real work is done in prolonged inquiry.

The journey is marked by three main steps. First, understanding and verifying our temperament and our type. Second, accepting that we are made with the urges we have subjectively verified. Acceptance is when we begin to change the way we live as a result of understanding. Third, loving the way we are made and enjoying the use of strengths and traits we were once trying to hide or avoid. Hiding them brought us no pleasure, only a sense of protection and being like others, at best. When all three steps have been taken, then we continue the journey that ends in reaching our full potential, which occurs the day after we die!

May your life be rich with understanding and made whole with acceptance and love as you walk this path. We have other literature and helps that you may want to explore listed in the closing pages of this book. Know yourself.

Ray W. Lincoln

Appendices

Appendix I: *The Temperament Key for Adults*

Instructions

Both the Adult Temperament Key and Child Temperament Key used in *INNERKINETICS* have been developed using the principles of research into temperament that Myers-Briggs, Keirsey, and Harkey-Jourgensen have used for the development of their assessments. These principles, when used in assessments, have proved very reliable and can be depended upon.   Any of the above named assessments of temperament are excellent guides to the discovery of how you are made on the inside.

As long as you carefully follow the instructions for the Temperament Key presented here, you should get excellent results.

This is a very positive assessment. We are looking for your strengths, not your weaknesses.   There are no wrong answers since it is a self-evaluation. However, be as accurate as possible. Read these instructions carefully since a knowledgeable guide is not looking over your shoulder who you can't ask for help. It is imperative that you answer according to these instructions.

- Answer these questions according to your preferences (what you prefer), not according to what you think others would have you become.
- Answer each question individually. Don't try to be consistent.
- Aim to get through the key in about 15 minutes or less.
- Think carefully about each answer; but avoid over-thinking, which can lead to confusion. If you are over-thinking, ask yourself: "What am I the most?"
- Again, let me put it this way: You will see yourself as both (a) and (b) in some of the questions.   Your answer should be what you see yourself to be the most, or what you prefer the most.
- Your preferences are often different at home than at work. This can be due to the fact that at work certain things are required of you and, therefore, they have become your work preferences. You prefer to do it that way at work since that's what is good for you. If your work

preferences differ from your home preferences, answer according to your home preferences.

• We want to know what really beats in your breast, what really satisfies, fulfills or pleases you the most.

The results should be accurate, but if you attend one of my seminars ask to be checked again. It's a service we provide. When you read the descriptions of the temperaments in Appendix II, you will determine whether they match your results in the Temperament Key. If they do not match the descriptions, then you answered with something else in mind, and you will need to switch to the temperament most like you.

This check on your answers is very helpful. The ones who are most likely to be confused about themselves are the NFs. They are the complicated temperament and have the greatest difficulties in understanding themselves for that understandable reason. Now, proceed with careful thought.

Note: You may also go to our website at www.raywlincoln.com/ RESOURCES where you will find a free, downloadable Adult Temperament Key.

ADULT TEMPERAMENT KEY

Check (A) or (B) for each question. Please answer ALL questions.

1. At social gatherings do you prefer to
_____ A. Socialize with everyone
_____ B. Stick to your friends

2. Are you more in touch with
_____ A. The real world
_____ B. The world inside your mind; the world of possibilities

3. Do you rely more on, or take more notice of
_____ A. Your experiences
_____ B. Your hunches or gut feelings

4. Are you (most of the time)
_____ A. Cool, calm, and collected
_____ B. Friendly and warm

5. When evaluating people do you tend to be
_____ A. Impersonal and frank
_____ B. Personal and considerate

6. Do you mostly feel a sense of
_____ A. Urgency/upset if you are not on time
_____ B. Relaxed about time.

7. When you see a mess do you
_____ A. Have an urge to tidy it up
_____ B. Feel reasonably comfortable living with it

8. Would you describe yourself as
_____ A. Outgoing/demonstrative/easy to approach
_____ B. Somewhat reserved/private

9. Which are you best at
_____ A. Focusing on details
_____ B. Catching the big picture, the connections, the patterns

10. Children should be
_____ A. Made to be more responsible
_____ B. Encouraged to exercise their imagination and make-believe more

11. When making decisions, are you more influenced by
_____ A. The facts or impersonal data
_____ B. Personal feelings

12. Do you feel more yourself when giving
_____ A. Honest criticism
_____ B. Support, approval, and encouragement

13. Do you work best
_____ A. Scheduled; to deadlines
_____ B. Unscheduled; no deadlines

14. For a vacation do you prefer to
_____ A. Plan ahead of time
_____ B. Choose as you go

15. When you are with others do you usually
_____ A. Initiate the conversation
_____ B. Listen and tend to be slow to speak

16. Most of the time, facts
_____ A. Should be taken at face value.
_____ B. Suggest ideas, possibilities, or principles.

17. Do you mostly feel
_____ A. In touch with the real world
_____ B. Somewhat removed, lost in thought

18. When in an argument or discussion do you care more about
_____ A. Defending your position and being right
_____ B. Finding harmony and agreement

19. With others do you tend to be
_____ A. Firm
_____ B. Gentle

20. Do you see yourself as
_____ A. Predictable
_____ B. Unpredictable

21. Do you mostly prefer to
_____ A. Get things done; come to closure
_____ B. Explore alternatives; keep options open

22. After two hours at a party are you
_____ A. More energized than when you arrived
_____ B. Losing your energy

23. Which best describes you
_____ A. Down to earth, practical
_____ B. Imaginative, an idea person

24. Which do you finally rely on more
_____ A. Common sense
_____ B. Your intuition/insights or your own analysis

25. In other people, which appeals to you most
_____ A. A strong will
_____ B. Warm emotions

26. Are you more controlled by
_____ A. Your head/thought
_____ B. Your heart/emotions

27. Are you typically
_____ A. Eager to get decisions made
_____ B. Not keen on making decisions

28. On the whole do you spend your money
_____ A. Cautiously
_____ B. Impulsively

29. When you have lost energy, do you find yourself mostly
_____ A. Seeking out people
_____ B. Seeking out solitude/a quiet corner

30. Do dreamers
_____ A. Annoy you somewhat
_____ B. Fascinate and interest you

31. Do you rely more
_____ A. On your five senses
_____ B. On your sixth sense/intuition

32. Are you more
_____ A. Tough-minded
_____ B. Tenderhearted

33. Would you more likely choose to be
_____ A. Truthful
_____ B. Tactful

34. Do you see yourself as more
_____ A. Serious and determined
_____ B. Relaxed and easygoing

35. Do you feel more comfortable when
_____ A. Things are decided
_____ B. Your options are still open

36. Would you say you mostly
_____ A. Show your feelings readily
_____ B. Are private about your feelings and keep them inside

37. Would you prefer
_____ A. To be in touch with reality
_____ B. To exercise a creative imagination

38. Is your way of thinking more
_____ A. Conventional
_____ B. Original and creative

39. What motivates you more
_____ A. Solid evidence
_____ B. An emotional appeal

40. *Would you rather be known for*
_____ A. *Being a consistent thinker*
_____ B. *Having harmonious relationships*

41. *Do you tend to*
_____ A. *Value routines*
_____ B. *Dislike routines*

42. *Do you live more with*
_____ A. *A little sense of urgency*
_____ B. *A leisurely pace*

43. *Do you have*
_____ A. *Many friends and count them all your close friends*
_____ B. *Few friends, and only one or two that are deep friends*

44. *Do you place more emphasis on what you see*
_____ A. *With your physical eyes*
_____ B. *With your mind's eye*

45. *Are you*
_____ A. *Thick skinned; not hurt easily*
_____ B. *Thin skinned; hurt easily*

46. *When you are asked to create a "To Do" list, does it*
_____ A. *Seem like the right thing to do and do you feel it will be helpful*
_____ B. *Bug you and seem more like an unnecessary chore*

47. *Which word attracts you most or describes you best?*
_____ A. *Talkative*
_____ B. *Quiet*

48. *Which words attract you most or describe you best?*
_____ A. *Present realities*
_____ B. *Future hopes*

49. *Which word(s) attracts you most or describe(s) you best?*
_____ A. *Logic*
_____ B. *Loving heart*

50. *Which word attracts you most or describes you best?*
_____ A. *Plan*
_____ B. *Impulse*

51. *Which word attracts you most or describes you best?*
_____ A. *Party*
_____ B. *Home*

52. *Which word(s) attracts you most or describe(s) you best?*
_____ A. *Common sense*
_____ B. *Vision*

53. *Which word attracts you most or describes you best?*
_____ A. *Justice*
_____ B. *Mercy*

54. *Which word attracts you most or describes you best?*
_____ A. *Concerned*
_____ B. *Carefree*

SCORE SHEET

Instructions:

1. Place an ☒ in the appropriate column (A or B) to indicate the answer you chose for each numbered question. [Please note that the numbers run from left to right across the chart.]
2. Count the number of "As" in column #1 and write that number in box "c" (above the "E"). Count the number of "Bs" in column #1 and write that number in box "d" (above the "I").
3. Count the number of "As" in column #2 and write that number in box "e." Count the number of "Bs" in column #2 and write that number in box "f."
4. Count the number of "As" in column #3 and write that number box "g." Count the number of "Bs" in column #3 and write that number in box "h."
5. Add the number of "As" for columns 2 and 3 together and write the total in box "i." Add the number of "Bs" for columns 2 and 3 and write that number in box "j."
6. Repeat the steps in instructions 3-5 above for columns 4/5 and 6/7.
7. Which did you have more of, "Es" or "Is"? _____

Which did you have more of, "Ss" or "Ns"? _____
Which did you have more of, "Ts" or "Fs"? _____
Which did you have more of, "Js" or "Ps"? _____

8. *In the four letters you listed in Instruction #7, which two-letter combination below is present? Circle it!*

S and P   S and J   N and T   N and F

	1		2		3		4		5		6		7
	A	B	A	B	A	B	A	B	A	B	A	B	A	B
1		2		3		4		5		6		7	
8		9		10		11		12		13		14	
15		16		17		18		19		20		21	
22		23		24		25		26		27		28	
29		30		31		32		33		34		35	
36		37		38		39		40		41		42	
43		44			45			46			
47		48			49			50			
51		52			53			54			

		g	h		m	n		s	t
		e	f		k	l		q	r
c	d	i	j		o	p		u	v
E	I	S	N		T	F		J	P

Appendix II: Short Descriptions of Each Temperament

These short descriptions will give you a quick idea of what the temperaments look like in real life. Check your Temperament Key results against these descriptions. If the descriptions are a brief description of you, then you have identified your temperament. If not, redo the Temperament Key, paying particular attention to the instructions.

Refer to the fuller descriptions in *INNERKINETICS* if the brevity of these do not suffice.

SP

They crave action, excitement, and stimulation, be it in sport, physical skills with the use of tools of all kinds, the performing arts, or even fine art. They are after a "good time" and only the introverted ones can happily sit still. They love freedom and act spontaneously. Therefore, they do not take to authority with relish. They have a natural talent for all things physical. They are lovable, exciting, adventuresome, and brave risk-takers.

SJ

They are hardworking with a responsible work ethic, and they crave a feeling of security, which makes them somewhat cautious in their adventures. They coined the motto "Be prepared." Home, family, and responsibilities, all cast around rules and regulations, make them feel comfortable. They are the solid citizens and the backbone of society. They feel a sense of duty and feel drawn to be useful.

NT

We could call this one the ingenious or technology temperament. They are curious and inventive, often finding their way into technology, science, and engineering occupations. They want to understand everything and build things. Often they are driven and compulsive, but display few people skills naturally. They are hardworking if what they are doing interests them. Feelings are not worn on the surface. NTs want to find new ways of doing things.

NF

They care very deeply about people and their world. They are very passionate, tender, loving, and want to please. Their inner world is thwart with struggles and they are the influencers of society. Often finding their way into higher education (as do the NTs) and writing, they champion causes that benefit society and provide for personal growth. They long to better themselves and to help others to be all that they can be. They are complicated and easily hurt, with emotions very near the surface.

Passionate About Potential!

You may have already begun telling others as you experienced success from the understanding and skills you have acquired here. So if you are passionate about your new understanding, here are some ways you can help others to discover their own purpose and potential. Who knows, you might help to change the world!

1. Give the book to friends as a gift. They need a magnificent glimpse into the wonderful way they are made.
2. If you have a website or blog, consider commenting about the book and how it has helped you – and maybe how it has helped the lives of others you know.
3. Write a book review for your local paper, favorite magazine, newsletter or a website you frequent.
4. Ask your favorite radio show or podcast host to invite Ray as a guest. (Journalists and media representatives often give attention to the requests from their watchers, readers, and listeners.)
5. If you own a shop or business, consider putting a display of the books on your counter to resell to customers. The books are available at a discounted rate for resale. For individuals, we offer a volume discount pricing for six books or more. Please contact us for details.
6. Buy several books and provide them to shelters, prisons, rehabilitation homes, and such where people may need help connecting with themselves.
7. Talk about the book in your e-mails, groups, clubs, forums you frequent, and other places where you engage in conversation, whether in person or on the internet. Share how the book has helped you and others, and offer people the link to the Ray W. Lincoln web site, www.raywlincoln.com.
8. If you know of people (authors, speakers, etc.) who have websites, blogs or newsletters, ask them if they would review a copy and make some comments about it to their audience, fans, and subscribers.

We welcome your comments and success stories. You can send them to info@raywlincoln.com. Implement the power of your *InnerKinetics*®!

About the Author

RAY W. LINCOLN

Ray W. Lincoln is the bestselling author of I'M a KEEPER and is the founder of Ray W. Lincoln & Associates. Ray's is a professional life coach and an expert in human nature. His 40 plus years of experience in speaking, teaching, and counseling began in New Zealand and have carried him to Australia and the United States. He speaks with energy and enthusiasm before large and small audiences. It was not by accident that he became the international speaker and coach that he is today and acquired the ability to guide so many to a happier, healthier, more fulfilled life. Ray has studied extensively in the fields of Philosophy, Temperament Psychology, and Personology. A member of the National Speakers Association, his expertise has been used as a lecturer and professor, teacher and keynote speaker, seminar presenter, counselor, and coach. He teaches and leads in staff trainings, university student retreats, and parents' educational classes, as well as other seminars and training events. He also trains and mentors teachers and other professionals and executives — all with the goal of understanding our own temperaments and those of others.

Ray lives with his wife, Mary Jo, in Littleton, Colorado where they enjoy hiking, snowshoeing, fly fishing, and all the beauty the Rocky Mountains offer. Both are highly involved in their work (which they feel is the most important and most fulfilling work of their entire career lives), both filling the roles for which they were designed, as they travel to speak to groups and to present seminars and workshops throughout the US.

<www.innerkinetics.com> Our website is a great place to order additional copies of **INNERKINETICS**

We also have additional FREE resources there to help you. Before you go to www.innerkinetics.com, however, go to:

www.raywlincoln.com

At this website you can:
- Sign up for our FREE monthly newsletter, which entitles you to:
- Receive 15% off all purchases at www.innerkinetics.com, www.imakeeperkid.com , and www.raywlincoln.com.
- Receive a FREE .pdf download of Ray's article, *Leveraging the Power of Your Mind.*

Find more helpful resources and information about our services.

OUR SERVICES INCLUDE Professional Life Coaching Educational Seminars and Training Keynote Addresses Educational Materials Free Monthly Newsletter

MY NOTES

MY NOTES

CPSIA information can be obtained at www.ICGtesting.com
Printed in the USA
LVOW05s1140201213

365882LV00001B/17/P